impact

3

SERIES EDITORS
JoAnn (Jodi) Crandall
Joan Kang Shin

AUTHOR
Diane Pinkley

NATIONAL GEOGRAPHIC LEARNING | CENGAGE Learning

Australia • Brazil • Mexico • Singapore • United Kingdom • United States

Thank you to the educators who provided invaluable feedback during the development of *Impact*:

EXPERT PANEL

Márcia Ferreira, Academic Coordinator, CCBEU, Franca, Brazil

Jianwei Song, Vice-general Manager, Ensure International Education, Harbin, China

María Eugenia Flores, Academic Director, and **Liana Rojas-Binda**, Head of Recruitment & Training, Centro Cultural
    Costarricense-Norteamericano, San José, Costa Rica

Liani Setiawati, M.Pd., SMPK 1 BPK PENABUR Bandung, Bandung, Indonesia

Micaela Fernandes, Head of Research and Development Committee and Assessment Committee,
    Pui Ching Middle School, Macau

Héctor Sánchez Lozano, Academic Director, and **Carolina Tripodi**, Head of the Juniors Program, Proulex,
    Guadalajara, Mexico

Rosario Giraldez, Academic Director, Alianza Cultural, Montevideo, Uruguay

REVIEWERS

BRAZIL

Renata Cardoso, Colégio do Sol, Guara, DF

Fábio Delano Vidal Carneiro, Colégio Sete de Setembro, Fortaleza

Cristiano Carvalho, Centro Educacional Leonardo da Vinci, Vitória

Silvia Corrêa, Associação Alumni, São Paulo

Carol Espinosa, Associação Cultural Brasil Estados Unidos, Salvador

Marcia Ferreira, Centro Cultural Brasil Estados Unidos, Franca

Clara Haddad, ELT Consultant, São Paulo

Elaine Carvalho Chaves Hodgson, Colégio Militar de Brasília, Brasília

Thays Farias Galvão Ladosky, Associação Brasil América, Recife

Itana Lins, Colégio Anchieta, Salvador

Samantha Mascarenhas, Associação Cultural Brasil
    Estados Unidos, Salvador

Ann Marie Moreira, Pan American School of Bahia, Bahia

Rodrigo Ramirez, CEETEPS- Fatec Zona Sul, São Paulo

Paulo Torres, Vitória Municipality, Vitória

Renata Zainotte, Go Up Idiomas, Rio de Janeiro

CHINA

Zhou Chao, MaxEn Education, Beijing

Zhu Haojun, Only International Education, Shanghai

Su Jing, Beijing Chengxun International English School, Beijing

Jianjun Shen, Phoenix City International School, Guangzhou

COSTA RICA

Luis Antonio Quesada-Umaña, Centro Cultural Costarricense
    Norteamericano, San José

INDONESIA

Luz S. Ismail, M.A., LIA Institute of Language and Vocational
    Training, Jakarta

Selestin Zainuddin, LIA Institute of Language and Vocational
    Training, Jakarta

Rosalia Dian Devitasari, SMP Kolese Kanisius, Jakarta

JAPAN

John Williams, Tezukayama Gakuen, Nara

MEXICO

Nefertiti González, Instituto Mexicano Madero, Puebla

Eugenia Islas, Instituto Tlalpan, Mexico City

Marta MM Seguí, Colegio Velmont A.C., Puebla

SOUTH KOREA

Min Yuol (Alvin) Cho, Global Leader English Education, Yong In

THAILAND

Panitnan Kalayanapong, Eduzone Co., Ltd., Bangkok

TURKEY

Damla Çaltuğ, İELEV, Istanbul

Basak Nalcakar Demiralp, Ankara Sinav College, Ankara

Humeyra Olcayli, İstanbul Bilim College, Istanbul

VIETNAM

Chantal Kruger, ILA Vietnam, Hô Chí Minh

Ai Nguyen Huynh, Vietnam USA Society, Hô Chí Minh

impact

3

Scope and Sequence

  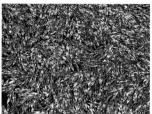 

	1 **Who Am I?** p. 8	**2** **Misunderstood Animals** p. 24	**3** **Everybody's Doing It!** p. 42	**4** **Fashion Footprints** p. 58
THEME	Teen identity and personality	Animals in popular culture	Human and animal group behavior	Making responsible fashion choices
VOCABULARY STRATEGY	· Suffix -ous · Using context	· Prefixes mis- and un- · Using a thesaurus	· Synonyms · Definitions and examples	· Suffix -al · Using a dictionary
SPEAKING STRATEGY	Comparing and contrasting	Expressing surprise and disbelief	Expressing cause and effect	Asking for clarification and clarifying
GRAMMAR	**Tag questions:** Confirming information or seeking agreement *Alicia is friendly, isn't she?* **Special uses of *it*:** *I hate it when the alarm goes off.*	**Modals:** Speculating about the past *He refuses to go in the water. He might have seen a jellyfish.* **Infinitives with and without *to*:** *He doesn't want to hold rats. Have him try it.*	**Separable and inseparable two-word verbs:** *They figured out a solution.* **Enough, too many, too much:** Talking about amounts: *I have enough pillowcases, but there are not enough feathers. I need more.*	**Present passive:** Describing actions and processes *A lot of pesticides are used to grow cotton.* **Modals:** Making suggestions and giving advice about present and past actions *You shouldn't have bought that leather jacket.*
READING	*Why Am I Me?*	*Vampire Bats - The Truth Exposed!*	*Humans in Groups*	*A Passion for Fashion*
READING STRATEGY	Identify descriptive words	Distinguish supporting details	Look for definitions and examples	Compare and contrast
VIDEO	*What Makes Up an Identity?*	*Face-to-Face with a Leopard Seal*	*Smarter by the Swarm*	*How Your T-Shirt Can Make a Difference*
MISSION	**Be Determined** National Geographic Explorer: **Jack Andraka**, Inventor	**Keep an Open Mind** National Geographic Explorer: **Jenny Daltry**, Herpetologist and Conservationist	**Collaborate** National Geographic Explorer: **Iain Couzin**, Behavioral Ecologist	**Your Choices Count** National Geographic Explorer: **Asher Jay**, Creative Conservationist
WRITING	Genre: **Comparison and contrast essay** Focus: Compare	Genre: **Process description** Focus: Describe purpose and sequence	Genre: **Descriptive essay** Focus: Give examples	Genre: **Persuasive essay** Focus: Introduce facts and opinion
PRONUNCIATION	Intonation in tag questions	Modals + *have* + past participle	Pausing	*Shouldn't have* + past participle
EXPRESS YOURSELF	Creative Expression: **Flash fiction** *A Day in the Life*		Creative Expression: **Poem** *The Garb Age*	
	Making connections: Teen identity and misunderstood animals		Making connections: Fashion trends and group behavior	

 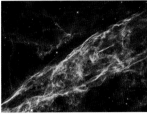  

Unit 1

JACK ANDRAKA **Inventor**

When Jack Andraka was 15 years old, he invented a test to detect certain types of cancer. Jack hopes he can inspire other young people to pursue their passions. He believes that everyone has the power to make a difference. What are you passionate about?

Unit 2

JENNY DALTRY **Herpetologist and Conservationist**

Jenny Daltry has always loved reptiles. She collected lizards, frogs, and snakes near her home when she was a child. She also volunteered at a zoo. When Jenny was 18, she traveled to India to work on a crocodile farm. There she realized she wanted to become a herpetologist: someone who studies reptiles.

Unit 3

IAIN COUZIN **Behavioral Ecologist**

Iain Couzin uses math to study how animals behave in groups. With mathematical models, he can take a closer look at bird migrations, insect colonies, and schools of fish. Iain thinks we can use this research to answer questions about our world, such as "How do animals benefit from working in groups?" and "Can humans learn from animal behavior to work better in groups?"

Unit 4

ASHER JAY **Creative Conservationist**

Do you think about where your clothes come from? Asher Jay does! She paints, writes, and designs fashions that help raise awareness for sustainability and conservation. Asher feels very connected to the environment and to all living things, even plants and bugs. That's why she wants to reduce her fashion footprint and inspire others to do the same.

Unit 5

RYAN CARNEY Paleontologist/Evolutionary Biologist

Ryan Carney's hero is Leonardo da Vinci. Most people know that da Vinci was a painter and an architect. Did you know that he also designed flying machines? Ryan is a little like his hero. He's also an artist, and studies the evolution of flight. Ryan examines flying dinosaurs and compares them with modern-day birds using x-ray machines.

Unit 6

BETHANY EHLMANN Planetary Geologist

Bethany Ehlmann studies planets and explores our solar system and beyond. She works on the NASA Mars Rover Curiosity mission. Bethany helps Curiosity navigate to collect rocks and minerals on Mars. She hopes we can study these samples to find signs of life on Mars and on other worlds. Do you believe there's life beyond Earth?

Unit 7

AMI VITALE National Geographic Photographer

Ami Vitale is more than just a photographer—she's a visual storyteller. Ami has visited more than 90 countries to take photographs. She's lived in mud huts, interacted with giant pandas, and traveled through war zones. Ami thinks photos have the power to tell stories and create change. Do you enjoy taking photos? What story would you like to tell?

Unit 8

PAUL D. MILLER AKA DJ SPOOKY Artist/Writer/Musician

Artist, writer, and musician Paul D. Miller performs under the name DJ Spooky. He uses technology to create unique blends of sound for his songs. He's developed a DJ app to let others do the same. Paul looks at music as information, not just sound. He hopes his musical compositions can raise awareness about environmental and social issues.

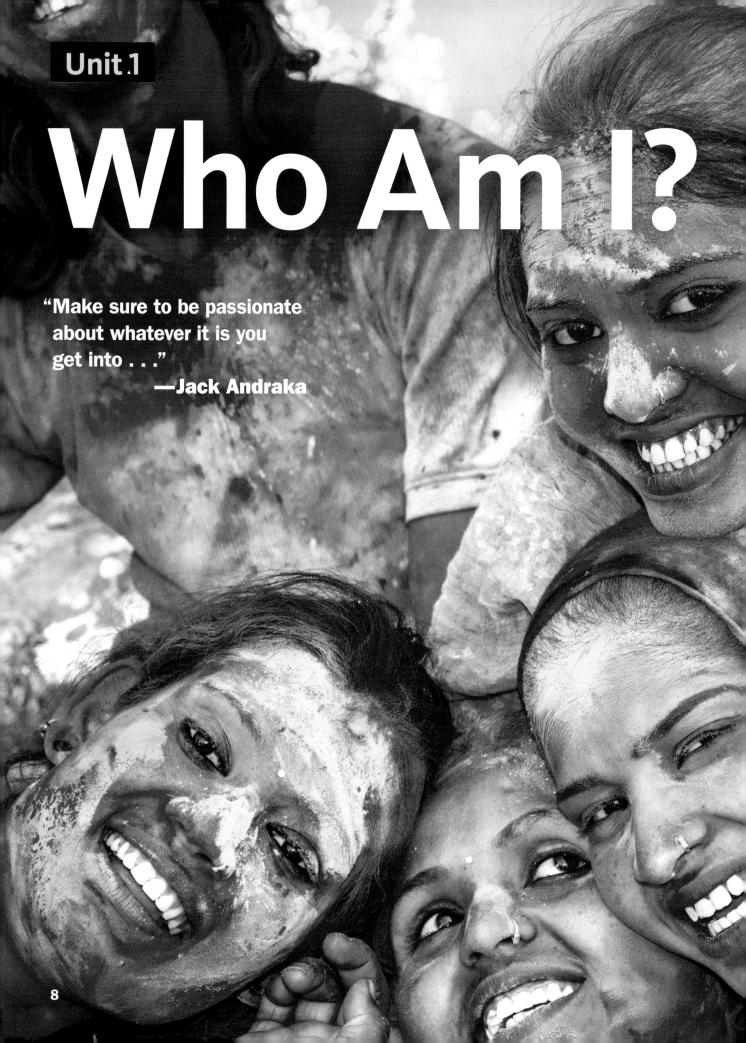

Who Am I?

"Make sure to be passionate about whatever it is you get into . . ."

—Jack Andraka

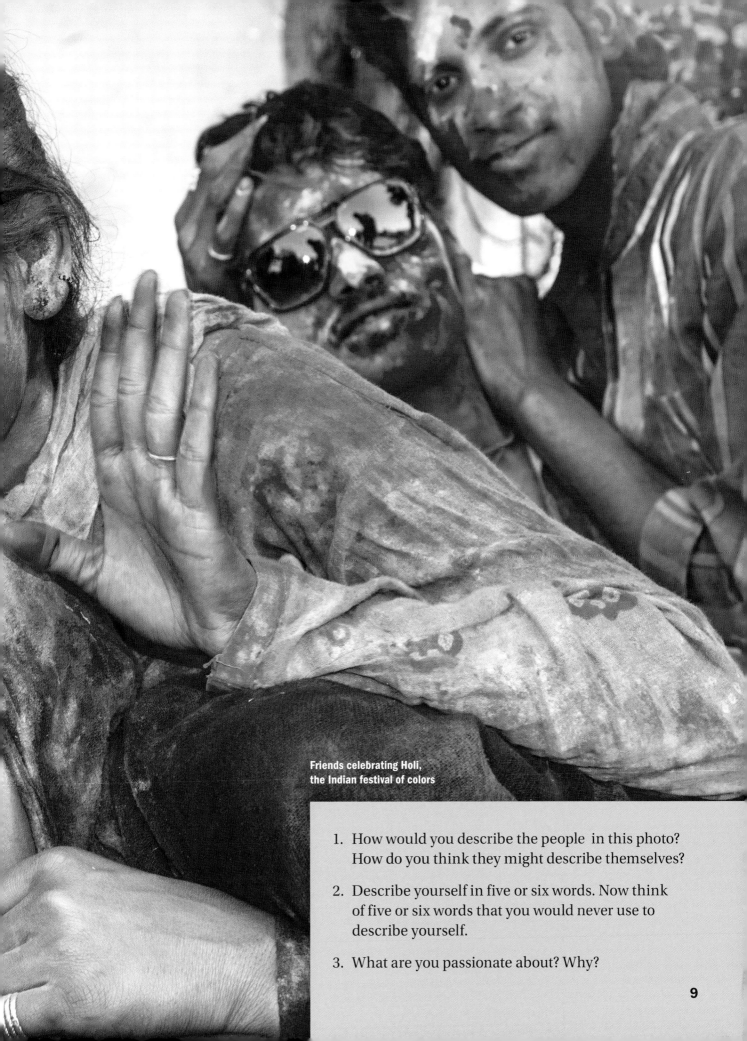

Friends celebrating Holi,
the Indian festival of colors

1. How would you describe the people in this photo? How do you think they might describe themselves?

2. Describe yourself in five or six words. Now think of five or six words that you would never use to describe yourself.

3. What are you passionate about? Why?

For teenagers, life can seem exciting and confusing at the same time, can't it? As a teenager, you're on your way to becoming an adult. It's a time of important changes and important questions.

A lot of these questions are about **identity**, or who you are. You're an individual, but you're also a product of your family life, your social environment, and your culture. Your identity includes your beliefs, your values, and your actions. You learned your values from your family, but, as a teenager, you may become less interested in what your family thinks. You may choose to spend more time with other people whose values and personalities are like yours. That's natural.

Then there's **personality**, or the qualities that make you different from other people. If you love parties and are **enthusiastic** about meeting lots of new people, you're probably **outgoing** and **self-confident**. If you get excellent grades in school, chances are you're **organized** and **responsible**. If you're **energetic** or adventurous, you might like hiking, or getting together with friends to explore a cave! If you're **optimistic**, **generous**, and **patient**, you might enjoy helping by spending time with animals at a shelter, or by participating in a local clean-up event.

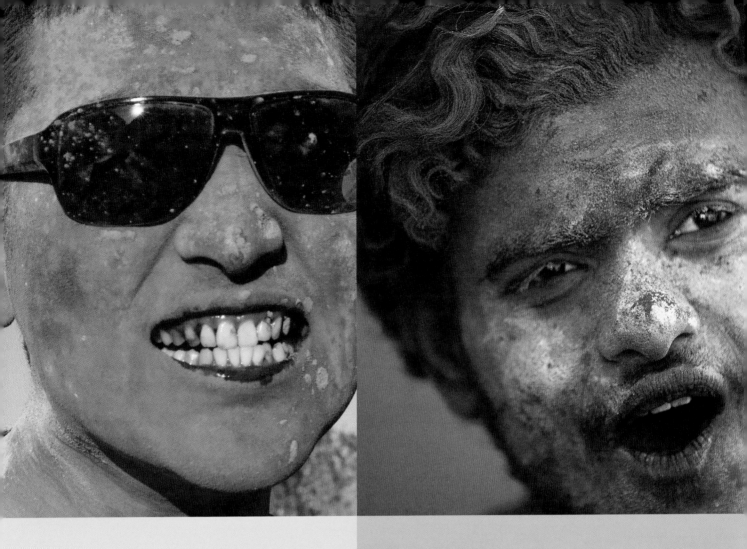

Personality is tricky. You might assume that everyone sees you the way you see yourself, but that isn't always true. Friends may laugh at your stories and think you have a great **sense of humor**, but your brother might think you're just odd. You may see yourself as **ambitious** because you're **determined** to get what you want, but others may feel you're stubborn, or unwilling to take advice. You may feel self-conscious and **shy**, while other people may think you're unfriendly. You may think you're fair, but you may still seem unreasonable or unkind to a friend.

Understanding yourself and how others see you can really be a puzzle!

2 **Learn new words.** Listen and repeat. TR: 3

3 **Work in pairs.** Make another list of five or six words that describe you, using the new vocabulary. Then make a list of five or six words that describe your partner. Compare your lists. Do you agree with your partner's description of you? Why or why not?

11

4 Read and write the words from the list.

ambitious	determined	enthusiastic	generous
optimistic	organized	outgoing	self-confident

By the time Jack Andraka was 14 years old, he was very _____ about science. Jack really wanted to focus on cancer research. He came up with a cheap, fast way to detect a type of cancer. When he first proposed his idea, some adults thought that Jack was being too _____ , but he was _____ to prove them wrong. He stayed _____ and entered his idea into an international science fair. Jack won! Now he feels more _____ . People have even asked him to be on TV because of his _____ personality and creative ideas.

5 Learn new words. Listen for the words. Write each trait next to the correct example. Are these words positive or negative? Decide. Then, listen and repeat. TR: 4 and 5

2014 Emerging Explorer, inventor Jack Andraka

fair	odd	self-conscious	stubborn

_____ 1. You never change! Just listen to me for once.

_____ 2. You put salt and pepper on your ice cream? Wow!

_____ 3. I like our music teacher. In her class, everyone gets a chance to play.

_____ 4. Oh, come on. Nobody is looking at you. Let's dance.

6 Choose an activity. Work in pairs.

1. Together, think of a famous person, such as a singer, actor, or Internet personality. Separately, list as many descriptive words as you can about that person. Are any of your words the same? Do you agree with your partner's description?

2. As a student, you're an expert on teachers. Think about teachers you've had, and write words to describe them. Look at the positive qualities you both listed. Then work together to write a description of your ideal teacher.

3. Write the letters in your partner's name going down the side of a paper. Then write a word that describes your partner for each letter. When you're finished, compare your name poems. Do you agree with your partner's description?

Musical
Ambitious
Responsible
Curious
Organized

SPEAKING STRATEGY TR: 6

Comparing	Contrasting
You're <u>outgoing</u>? So am I!	You're <u>shy</u>? Not me! I'm not <u>shy</u> at all.
Just like you, I'm <u>self-confident</u>.	Unlike you, I'm <u>optimistic</u>.
We're alike because we're both <u>patient</u>.	I'm <u>determined</u>, but you're just <u>stubborn</u>!

7 **Listen.** How do the speakers compare and contrast their little brothers? Write the words and phrases you hear. **TR: 7**

8 **Read and complete the dialogue.**

Dave: My aunt and uncle are visiting this week.

Nina: You don't seem very happy about it.

Dave: I'm not. My aunt is always saying, "You're _____ your uncle Jack!"

Nina: Well, are you and your uncle _____ ?

Dave: No, we're very different. _____ _____ him, I'm active and outgoing. All he does is watch TV.

Nina: Is he funny? Optimistic? Generous, _____ you?

Dave: No way. _____ ! He never gives me anything, not even on my birthday.

9 **Work in pairs.** Take turns. Use a coin to move. (Heads = 1 space; tails = 2 spaces) Compare and contrast as instructed.

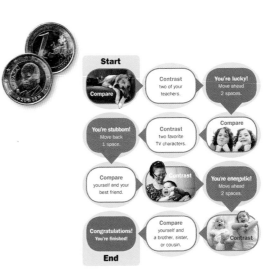

10 **Work in groups.** Compare and contrast your parents. Are you like or unlike your parents? Do your classmates' parents seem like or unlike your own parents?

Go to p. 153.

13

GRAMMAR TR: 8

Tag questions: Confirming information or seeking agreement

Alicia **is** friendly, **isn't she**?	Yes. She's outgoing. You'll like her.
You**'re** nervous about the competition, **aren't you**?	I am. I'm not sure I'm ready.
Rick **doesn't** live near here, **does he**?	No, he doesn't. He lives pretty far away.
Lin also **plays** the flute, **doesn't she**?	Yes, she does. She's really good!
Sue **couldn't** make herself do it, **could she**?	No. She's too shy.

11 **Listen.** Match the questions to logical answers. Write the letter. TR: 9

1. _____ a. Yes, it was. And we finally won!

2. _____ b. Yes, I have to be. I'm a teacher.

3. _____ c. No, she didn't. She said she was sick.

4. _____ d. He really is. He never stops!

5. _____ e. Yes, she can. And the guitar, too.

12 **Read.** Then complete the tag questions.

1. Carla and Lea want to join the team, _____*don't they*_____ ?

2. You're not as enthusiastic about poetry as your sister, _____ ?

3. Greg's brothers won't be at the party, _____ ?

4. Maria has changed a lot, _____ ? She's so self-confident.

5. Your sisters didn't go shopping, _____ ?

6. You would help us if Ana can't come, _____ ?

**National Geographic Fellow
Chef Barton Seaver**

13 **Work in pairs.** Take turns forming tag questions and answering them. Agree or disagree with your partner. Express your opinion.

1. (name of a place) / most beautiful / place / ever
2. (name of a singer) / most popular / singer / right now
3. (name of an actor) / talented / actor / on TV
4. (name of a video game) / your favorite / video game
5. (name of a movie) / exciting / movie / ever

Barton Seaver is the most interesting chef around, isn't he?

Yes, he really is. He has great ideas about food.

14

14 **Learn new words.** Read about young chefs, and listen to their conversations. Then listen and repeat.   TR: 10 and 11

Everyone loves cooking shows! The chefs are usually self-confident and energetic, but they're not always patient or organized, are they? (That's part of the fun!) They're almost always very **competitive** as they cook against each other. They want to win by making the best food they can!

On some shows, teen chefs compete to see who's the best cook. These teen chefs can be surprisingly **cooperative**, even while they're competing. They've made friends, and they're interested in what one another is doing. Of course, one chef may be **jealous** of another chef, but in the end many of them are still **helpful** and kind to each other as they compete. They're **open-minded** enough to know that only one person can win, but all of them can be friends—and great chefs.

15 **Read.** Then use a tag question to comment.

1. Angela really is a talented cook. I want to be like her!

    You aren't feeling jealous, are you?

2. Pat and Tim refused to talk to Julia, or even listen to her ideas.

   _____

3. The Whitley twins have seventeen tennis trophies between them.

   _____

4. Sam won't join the group to help collect and recycle plastic bottles.

   _____

5. Here, let me help you clean up those dishes.

   _____

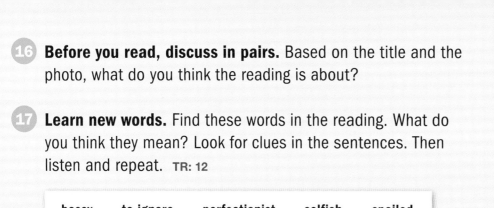

16 **Before you read, discuss in pairs.** Based on the title and the photo, what do you think the reading is about?

17 **Learn new words.** Find these words in the reading. What do you think they mean? Look for clues in the sentences. Then listen and repeat. TR: 12

| bossy | to ignore | perfectionist | selfish | spoiled |

18 **While you read, notice descriptive words you think apply to you personally.** TR: 13

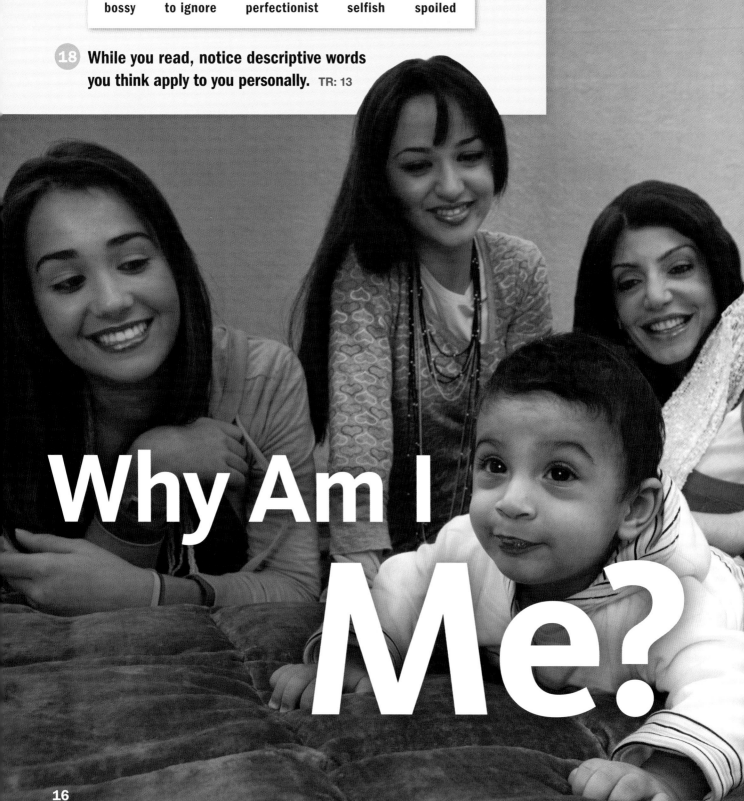

Why Am I Me?

Have you ever wondered why you are the way you are? What makes you different from, say, your brothers and sisters?

People have asked these questions for centuries, and researchers are trying to answer them. One idea they're exploring is that birth order influences the person we become. In general, the oldest child is described as confident, organized, dutiful, and determined to get what he or she wants. Oldest children are seen as born leaders, people-pleasers, and perfectionists. Because they're the oldest, their younger brothers and sisters sometimes see them as bossy, or too willing to tell other people what to do.

The middle child may be described as being competitive in order to get more attention. They sometimes feel that their family ignores them because they are in the middle. Because middle children tend to avoid conflict, they can be flexible and easygoing. They may also be seen as secretive by members of their family. They are usually more influenced by their friends than by their family, perhaps because they get more attention from their friends.

The youngest child is described as the baby of the family. They can be spoiled by their parents, who spend a lot of time with them and often give them what they want. For this reason, their brothers and sisters sometimes get jealous. Youngest children enjoy being the center of attention, and they are seen as outgoing, open-minded, and likely to take risks.

What if you're an only child? Many people think that a child with no brothers or sisters grows up wanting lots of attention. Some think they're selfish, or unwilling to share with others. But because they spend so much time around adults, they're also described as confident, determined, and responsible.

19 **After you read, discuss the questions in groups.**

1. What's the main idea of the reading?

2. Does birth order seem like a good way to describe personality? Why or why not?

3. Based on your personal experience, does the information in this reading seem correct? If not, why not?

20 **Work in pairs.** Separately, go back through the reading and underline all the words you think describe you. Then read your list to your partner. Based on your list, can your partner guess your birth order? What is it?

21 **Work in groups.** What other factors might affect your personality? Write two or three ideas. Briefly explain how each factor on your list might affect you. Then discuss your ideas in groups.

22 **Before you watch, discuss in pairs.** Look at the photo. What do the group members' clothes say about their identity?

23 **Work in pairs.** The video you are going to watch is called *What Makes Up an Identity?* From the title, predict the main idea of the video. Circle the correct letter.

a. The video will discuss your identity in comparison to that of your family and friends.

b. The video will talk about things that you like and do that help shape your identity.

c. The video will suggest ways you can make yourself better.

Rea Iktetsa Pantsula, a dance group from Soweto, Johannesburg, South Africa

24 Watch scene 1.1. **While you watch, check the factors that the video says are important parts of your identity.**

☐ sports ☐ clothes ☐ gadgets ☐ food

☐ music ☐ house ☐ pets ☐ other people

25 **After you watch, work in pairs.** Circle the correct letter.

1. According to the research, music can make us happier and _____ .

   a. smarter b. more organized c. more determined

2. A personal style is important to help you _____ .

   a. fit in b. stand out c. both a and b

3. One in _____ teens is obsessed with wearing designer clothing.

   a. two b. four c. twenty

4. Nearly all teenagers associate _____ with happy memories.

   a. music b. clothes c. food

5. Parents help _____ .

   a. influence our world view b. choose our friends c. choose our music

26 **Work in pairs.** The video describes four main areas that make up your identity. Discuss each of those areas in your own life.

27 **Discuss in groups.** At the end of the video, you're asked, "What else makes you *you*?" Answer the question in your group. Then share your responses with the class.

28 **Choose an activity.**

1. **Work independently.** Choose a classmate or teacher to interview about what makes up his or her identity. Write a profile of this person and share it with the class.

2. **Work in pairs.** Write a description of your clothing in relation to your identity. Have your partner do the same. Then compare your results. Does your partner have the same view of your style as you do? Discuss. Then switch roles.

3. **Work in groups.** Create a "happy memory" cookbook. Survey at least five classmates about meals that give them happy memories. Have the classmates describe the meals. Take notes, and then compile the information into a cookbook to share with the class.

Using *it* to talk about weather, time, and distance, and for emphasis

It's raining again. Another bad hair day!

It's six o'clock already. Wake up!

It's a half-mile walk from here. We're late!

It's weird that we've had so much rain.

I hate **it** when the alarm goes off.

It drives me crazy when I have to hurry.

---

29 **Listen.** How is *it* used? Write the number. TR: 15

_____ to introduce weather   _____ to introduce time

_____ to introduce distance   _____ to introduce emphasis

30 **Work in pairs.** Write down three things that you don't like to happen. Use *it* in your sentences. Then share them with your partner.

1. *It makes me a little angry when people interrupt me in a conversation.*

2. _____

3. _____

4. _____

31 **Work in pairs.** Write down three things that you like to happen. Use *it* in your sentences. Then share them with your partner.

1. *I like it when people give me compliments about my appearance.*

2. _____

3. _____

4. _____

32 **Work in groups.** Make the cube. Take turns tossing the cube and completing the sentences.

It drives me crazy when my friends don't return my texts!

It drives me crazy when...

It's nice that...

I love it when...

Go to p. 155.

20

WRITING

When we compare and contrast two people or things, we use phrases such as the following:

Compare:	**alike**	**both**	**in the same way**	**too**
Contrast:	**although**	**but**	**on the other hand**	**unlike**

33 **Read the model.** Work in pairs to identify the parts of the writing. How does the writer compare and contrast? Underline the words or phrases.

I come from a large family, and I share personality traits with several family members. But it's clear to me that I'm most like my grandfather, although we're different in some ways, too.

My grandfather and I both like to spend time outdoors. We both enjoy riding our bikes and watching sports. We're adventurous, too. I really like to go fishing with my grandfather. We'll catch our dinner together, then cook and eat it at our campsite. We both love nature. We're alike in that way. We also enjoy working in his garden to grow fruits and vegetables.

It's a different story when winter comes. Unlike my grandfather, I love being outside in the snow. I like to have snowball fights with my friends, but he likes to sit by the fire and read. Sometimes he and I play cards, although I don't really enjoy that very much. I'm too energetic to sit for so long! On the other hand, when we play one of my video games, I have fun because I'm competitive. My grandfather isn't competitive at all. He's also sort of slow!

But it doesn't really matter to me what we do together. I like being with my grandfather and spending time with him. We're a good fit!

34 **Work in pairs.** How are the writer and his grandfather alike? How are they different? Do you think they're more alike than different? Explain.

35 **Write.** Compare and contrast your personality with that of a family member.

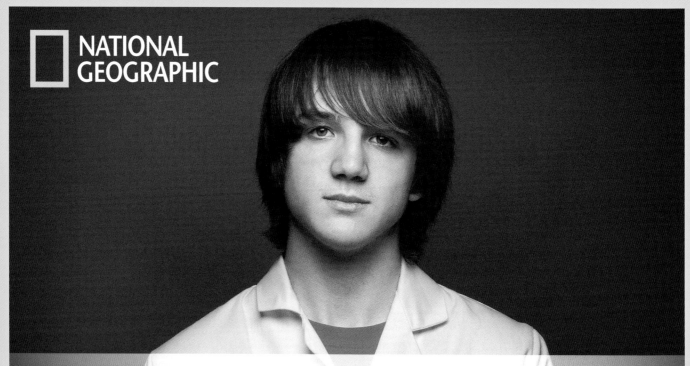

Be Determined

"Why not you? Why can't you come up with the next great innovation or cure?"
—Jack Andraka
National Geographic Explorer, Inventor

1. Watch scene 1.2.

2. It took Jack Andraka 4,000 tries to find a protein he needed for his experiment. It took him 200 tries to find a lab research scientist who would accept his project. What three words best describe Jack?

3. How hard do you try to get something you want or need? Do you give up easily? Would you try 200 times? 4,000 times? How would you feel if you were unsuccessful so many times?

Make an Impact

(A) **Plan and conduct a survey about personality traits.**

- Decide which traits you want to ask about. Include positive and negative traits.

- Write the survey.

- Interview ten people. Record and report the results.

(B) **Plan and write a report on other factors that influence personality.**

- Search the Internet for information on your topic.

- Write your report.

- Present your research to the class.

(C) **Write an advice column.**

- Write a letter to an advice columnist about a problem that young people face.

- In groups of three, read your letters aloud. Then discuss the problem and give advice. Take notes.

- Compile your group's questions and responses in an advice column. Make copies of your column to share with the class.

Misunderstood Animals

"Endangered snakes, frogs, and crocodiles are not everyone's favorites. They have a special need for attention."

—Jenny Daltry

A Nile crocodile carrying its young

1. How would you describe the animals in the photo?

2. What would you do if you saw a crocodile in the wild?

3. Of the three animals Jenny Daltry mentions, which do you like the least? Why?

1 **Why do we care about some animals but not others?** Discuss. Then listen and read.
TR: 16

Why are some animals popular while others are so unpopular? In the natural world, every animal has its place and purpose. Nature doesn't judge these animals—people do. For example, it's a common misconception that snakes are **slimy** and **disgusting** to touch. Not true! A snake's skin is smooth and dry. Another misconception is that snakes are **aggressive** and will attack humans for no reason. Also untrue! Almost all snakes, even **poisonous** ones, prefer to escape or hide unless they're surprised or attacked first. Snakes are very misunderstood animals.

Snakes aren't the only animals that are misunderstood. People think that cockroaches are dirty **pests** that like to hide in dark, **filthy** places. They hate the idea that cockroaches eat garbage and dead animals as they **decay**. People also believe cockroaches are covered in **germs**.

In fact, cockroaches clean themselves constantly, as much as cats do. They prefer to live in clean places. It's humans who, by trying to trap or **poison** cockroaches, force them to hide wherever they can in order to survive. Luckily for them, cockroaches are very hard to **destroy**. They were here on the planet before humans appeared, and they'll probably be here after we're gone!

A Borneo keeled pit viper

Cockroaches

26

A wasp

Wasps also have a bad reputation. Many people hate wasps because they believe that wasps **sting** humans at a moment's notice. Actually, most wasp species don't sting at all. Those that do sting are generally protecting their young, or responding to humans who yell or swing their hands at the wasp. Some wasp species do sting caterpillars, spiders, and other insects. When stinging, the wasps inject their eggs into their living prey. The wasp larvae live inside and, when they're ready to leave, they eat their way out!

Should we care about these misunderstood species? Yes, we should! Every animal species plays a **crucial** role in the **ecosystem**. Some help **control** other pest populations. Some help pollinate flowers. Some eat mildew and mold, and others protect food crops. Some help contribute to medical research. Even misunderstood animals are necessary, and in many ways they're **beneficial** to humans.

2 **Learn new words.** Listen and repeat.
TR: 17

3 **Work in pairs.** Did you like animals as a young child? Which animals were you afraid of? Describe them. Why were you afraid of them?

4 Read and write the words from the list.

beneficial	crucial	destroy	disgusting
ecosystem	poisonous	slimy	sting

A Siamese crocodile

At the age of eight, Jenny Daltry knew that she wanted to be a conservation biologist. She grew up collecting unusual animals, such as lizards, frogs, and snakes. Some people think such animals are _____ or _____ . But they play a _____ role in the _____ . For example, Siamese crocodiles live in Cambodia, where they dig out the marshes to hold water during the dry season. Some people want to _____ the crocodiles, but the water would dry up and other animals would have no water to drink. So, as Jenny Daltry reminds us, even scary crocodiles are _____ .

5 Learn new words. Listen for these words and match them to the definitions. Then listen and repeat. TR: 18 and 19

misconception	misunderstood	unpopular	untrue

_____ 1. not a fact

_____ 2. seen by others as different from how someone or something really is

_____ 3. not accepted by a large number of people

_____ 4. a wrong idea that people believe anyhow

6 Choose an activity.

1. **Work independently.** Choose one of the animals in the list below. Design a new look for the animal so that it doesn't seem so disgusting or unpleasant. What can you change? Think about the animal's size, color, and other physical details.

2. **Work in pairs.** Together, choose one of these animals: mosquitoes, rats, spiders, or worms. Separately, describe the animal in a word web. Then compare your word web with your partner's.

3. **Work in groups.** Rank the animals below from most misunderstood (1) to least misunderstood (5). Explain your group's ranking.

cockroaches	rats	snakes	spiders	wasps

SPEAKING STRATEGY TR: 20

Expressing surprise	Expressing disbelief
Wow! Really?	Oh, come on! You can't be serious.
That's <u>amazing</u>!	That's hard to believe.
No way! You're kidding!	Are you sure about that?

A blue-ringed octopus

7 **Listen.** How do the speakers express surprise and disbelief? Write the phrases you hear. TR: 21

8 **Read and complete the dialogue.**

John: This video game is full of fun facts about animals.

Mimi: Oh, really? Like what?

John: Like the fact that spiders have six or eight eyes.

Mimi: _____

John: Yeah, I'm sure. I looked it up. Here's another one. Honeybees die after their first sting.

Mimi: _____ Well, I know a fact about bees. They communicate through different dances.

John: _____ Look at this one about bees. They have hair on their eyes!

Mimi: _____ I know one about eyes. Did you know the colossal squid has eyes 30 cm (11 in.) wide?

John: _____

9 **Work in groups.** Cut out the cards. Take turns reading them aloud. Group members should express surprise or disbelief.

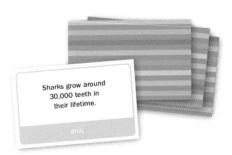

Sharks grow around 30,000 teeth in their lifetime.

10 **Work in pairs.** Take turns telling a surprising story about yourself that may be true or untrue. Your partner will express surprise or disbelief and then decide if your story is true or false.

Go to p. 157.

Modals: Speculating about the past

could have (not sure)	They canceled their hiking plans. They **could have read** about that escaped bear.
might have (not sure)	He refuses to go in the water. He **might have seen** a jellyfish.
may have (pretty sure)	She won't get out of the car now. She **may have heard** the neighbor's dogs fighting.
must have (very sure)	They took her to the hospital immediately. That spider **must have been** poisonous.

11 **Listen.** How sure are the speakers about their ideas? Write *not sure, pretty sure,* or *very sure.* TR: 23

1. _____   2. _____   3. _____

4. _____   5. _____   6. _____

12 **Read and write.** For each item, write a sentence speculating about the past. Use *could have, may have, might have,* and *must have* in your sentences.

1. Alice went into the kitchen for a midnight snack. She turned on the light and screamed. _____

2. Don kept scratching his arms and legs all night. _____
   _____

3. Julia heard something running inside the walls. _____
   _____

4. Ken found the trash can on its side. There was garbage all over the sidewalk.
   _____

13 **Work in pairs.** Take turns speculating about the past. Use *could have, may have, might have,* and *must have* in your sentences.

1. She cried all night.
2. They ran as fast as they could.
3. He got really angry.
4. She screamed after biting into her sandwich.

Caribbean giant cockroaches

14 Learn new words. Listen to information about spider bites. Then listen and repeat.
TR: 24 and 25

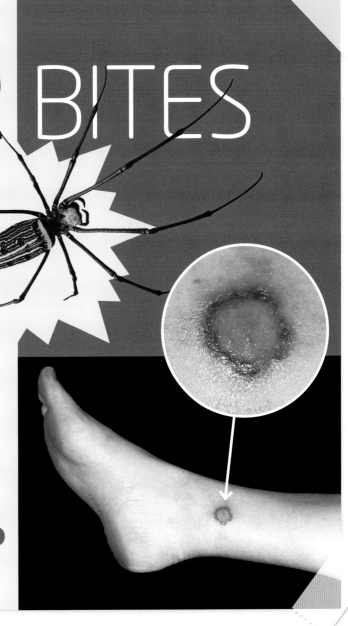

BE PREPARED.
SPIDER BITES

Are you **scared of** spider bites? Learn what to do.

- Do you have a spider **bite**?
- Spider bites can **hurt** a lot.
- Stay **calm.** Try not to get **upset**.
- If you think the bite is from a poisonous spider, don't move. Moving makes the **venom** go through your body faster.
- Wash the bite with soap and water. Then apply a cloth with cold water or ice to the bite.
- If the bite is on a hand, arm, or leg, keep the bite area above the level of your heart.

CALL FOR HELP IMMEDIATELY.

15 Work in pairs. Look at the poster again. The same advice is good for some scorpions, too. Take turns describing what to do if you're stung by a scorpion.

Emperor scorpion

16 Work in groups. Imagine that your friend showed you a bite on his arm. Speculate about what happened. Use *could have, may have, might have,* and *must have* in your sentences.

17 **Before you read, discuss in pairs.** What do you know about bats? Make a two-column chart. Write five things you think are true in the left-hand column.

18 **Learn new words.** Find these words in the reading. What do you think they mean? Use a thesaurus to check. Then listen and repeat. TR: 26

fangs	lethal	to lick	myth	to suck

19 **While you read, notice details that support the beliefs you listed in Activity 17.** TR: 27

20 **After you read, work in pairs to answer the questions.**

1. What is the main idea of the article?
2. How many species of bats are there?
3. What are some myths about bats?
4. Where do vampire bats get the blood they need?
5. How are vampire bats beneficial?

21 **Find details to support your beliefs.** Look at your chart from Activity 17. Next to each of your beliefs about bats, write any details from the reading that support those beliefs.

Vampire Bats
THE TRUTH EXPOSED!

ARE HUMANS RIGHT TO FEAR ALL THINGS VAMPIRE?

There are around 1,200 species of bats on the planet. Most of them eat insects or fruit. Some bats eat scorpions, frogs, or other small animals. But there are some bats that aren't interested in any of those foods. These are the often-feared vampire bats. And yes, it's true! Vampire bats do need to drink blood to survive!

Why are so many people scared of bats? They're scared in part because there are so many myths, or false stories, about bats. One myth is that bats are flying mice. Another is that bats are blind, and so they can get caught in your hair. But the most popular myth, by far, is the one that connects vampire bats and the scary, fictional creatures known as vampires.

In novels, films, and television shows, fictional vampires use their sharp fangs to bite people in the neck, and then suck their blood. Real vampire bats do have fangs. They use them to make small cuts in an animal's skin, but they don't suck blood through their fangs. Instead they wait until blood starts flowing from the cut. Then they lick up the blood with their tongues, just as a kitten drinks milk from a bowl.

Vampire bats get blood from birds, cows, horses, and other farm animals. They can drink gently from a sleeping animal for half an hour without waking it. Their bite isn't lethal, and the blood loss doesn't hurt the animals.

Vampire bats can live for about two days without drinking blood. This is usually plenty of time to look for food. And, unless there's no other food source available, a vampire bat won't bite a human. In general, vampire bats are comfortable, and sometimes even friendly, around humans.

In addition, vampire bats are a valuable source of information for medical research. While they're drinking blood, these bats release substances that help blood keep flowing as they drink. Scientists are studying vampire bats to see if they can develop medications that work in the same way. Their research could one day help people with circulation problems or medical conditions such as heart attacks and strokes.

22 Discuss in groups.

1. Even after they've learned that bats are beneficial, some people still don't like them. Why do you think that is?

2. Why do you think people like the idea of vampires so much? Do you have a favorite vampire character? Who is it? Why is this particular vampire your favorite?

23 **Before you watch, discuss in pairs.** Look at this photo. How would you feel if you were near this animal? What would you do?

24 **Write.** The video you're going to watch is called *Face-to-Face with a Leopard Seal*. From the title, predict what will happen when the photographer comes face-to-face with the animal in the photo.

_____

_____

_____

25 Watch scene 2.1. **While you watch, circle three words that are used in the video to describe the leopard seal.**

aggressive	big	nervous	predatory
caring	disgusting	terrified	useless

26 **After you watch, work in pairs to answer the questions.**

1. Where does the leopard seal live?
2. How does Paul Nicklen feel when he first gets into the water?
3. What does the leopard seal do to Paul to show a threat?
4. What does the leopard seal first bring to Paul?
5. Why does the leopard seal seem disgusted?
6. Why does Paul say that the leopard seal is panicked? What does she start doing at this point?
7. What are the misconceptions that Paul had about the animal? How does she change his ideas?

A leopard seal

27 **Work in pairs.** Look at your answers from Activity 24. Did you correctly predict the outcome of the video? Explain how the leopard seal's actions help classify it as a misunderstood animal.

28 **Discuss in groups.** Why do you think Paul wanted to photograph the leopard seal? What can he teach others about this animal with his photos and his story? Explain, using examples from the video.

29 **Choose an activity.**

1. **Work independently.** Research leopard seals. Learn about their role in the Antarctic ecosystem. What animals do they prey on? Who are their predators? Prepare a short presentation to share with the class.

2. **Work in pairs.** Compare and contrast the leopard seal with another misunderstood animal from this unit. Use a Venn diagram to show the two animals' similarities and differences.

3. **Work in groups.** Many people consider the leopard seal a dangerous, deadly predator. Create an advertisement to educate people about the leopard seal and persuade them to change their opinions.

GRAMMAR TR: 28

Infinitives with and without *to*

To hold a rat is scary!

He doesn't want **to hold** rats.

She's excited **to hold** one.

That's the rat **to get**!

She's going to the pet store **to buy** it.

I can't **hold** one!

Have him **try** it.

We'll watch her **do** it.

OK. I'll let her **buy** it.

I'll even help her **pay** for it.

---

30 **Read.** Circle the correct letter.

1. My brother really wants _____ get a pet rat.

   a. ⊘   b. to

2. My mother will absolutely not let him _____ buy one.

   a. ⊘   b. to

3. He's planning _____ save money for one anyway.

   a. ⊘   b. to

4. I can't wait _____ see what happens when Mom finds out.

   a. ⊘   b. to

5. She'll make him _____ take it back to the store.

   a. ⊘   b. to

6. I really like _____ see him get in trouble instead of me!

   a. ⊘   b. to

A rat

---

31 **Work in pairs.** Play Tic-Tac-Talk. Use infinitives with or without *to* in your sentences. One of you is X; the other is O.

I might touch a hairy spider!

Not me! I can't do it!

might	can't	have
make	want	help
watch	feel	ask

Ants

36

WRITING

A process description explains how something is done or how something happens. The purpose of the steps and the order in which they happen are described.

Purpose:	in order to	so that		
Sequence:	before	during	after	finally
	first	then	next	while
	little by little	meanwhile	over time	

32 **Read the model.** Work in pairs to identify the process being described. What words and phrases does the writer use to show purpose and sequence? Underline them.

When you're very, very afraid of something, that fear can affect you and how you live your life. When I was younger, I saw my cousin fall onto an ants' nest. The ants attacked him, and he was covered in horrible bites. After that, I became very scared of ants. I wouldn't eat outside, and I didn't even like to play outside. I checked my bed for ants every night. But when I turned thirteen, I decided I couldn't let my fear get to me. I had to learn to control my fear of ants.

First I read a lot about different ants. I didn't focus on bites, but instead I read about how beneficial ants are to the planet. Ants are really cool! They're hard-working, social, and organized. They help bring air and nutrients to the soil. They pollinate plants, clean up decaying matter, and help control other insects.

Next I began to watch ants from a safe distance. I started to look at a colony of ants in real time on the Internet in order to learn how they live. Little by little, I felt more comfortable about ants. Finally I went outside one day and let an ant crawl onto my hand. It was okay! Now that I know about all the good things ants do, I'm not so afraid of them anymore.

LIVE   Live feed of an ant farm

33 **Work in pairs.** Imagine you're scared of an insect or animal. What steps would you take if you wanted to control your fear? Why?

34 **Write.** Many people are scared of pit bulls. Imagine you have a new pit bull puppy. You don't want it to be misunderstood. How will you train it to be a good dog? Describe the process. How could you help people to understand your dog better?

Keep an Open Mind

"To me, it's symbolic. If you don't care about this particular snake, why should you care about anything else? Each one is part of a great web."

—Jenny Daltry

National Geographic Explorer, Herpetologist and Conservationist

1. **Watch scene 2.2.**

2. What can you do to learn more about misunderstood animals?

3. How can you help other people understand misunderstood animals?

Make an Impact

A Make a set of misunderstood-animal cards.

· Choose at least five misunderstood animals to research. Find two or three facts that might help clear up misunderstandings about the animals.

· Write information about the animal on one side of the card. Include a photo or drawing and caption on the other side.

· Present your cards to the class.

B Plan and produce an animal quiz show for TV.

· Decide on the format of your quiz show.

· Research and prepare questions about animals for competing teams.

· Act out and film the show.

C Educate others about misunderstood animals.

· Collect information about a group of misunderstood animals.

· Make informational posters or fact sheets.

· Display the posters in your school or hand out the fact sheets to students and teachers.

A jumping spider

Express Yourself

A Day in the Life

Well, finally something is happening, Kim thought. So far, it had been the most boring summer ever. School was starting in less than a week, and she had nothing interesting to report to her classmates. Suddenly, loud beeps—warning that a truck is backing up— broke the afternoon silence. Kim held her bottle of cold water against her forehead as she walked over to the bushes that separated her house from the one next door.

I hope the new neighbors are cool, she thought as she looked at the stacks of boxes outside the truck. *Let's see. Lots of boxes! That one says, "kitchen stuff," and that one says, "Jae's stuff." Wow, what a huge TV! Oh, a keyboard. I wonder who plays that. That box says, "Jae's trophies." Hmm. I wonder who Jae is. And look at that—a water dish with the name Cupcake on it.*

Maybe they have a cat, thought Kim. And then she saw a long pink leash tied to one of the handles on the back door of the truck. Whatever was on the other end of the leash was under the truck, staying out of the hot sun. And it probably wasn't a cat!

Kim stepped around the bushes to get a better look. "Here, Cupcake. Come here, girl!" she called. She poured some of her water into the dish and called again. "Here, Cupcake. Come on out, little girl."

Kim heard something move. A large dog crawled out from under the truck, and then stood up and shook itself. "Well, look at you," Kim said. "You're not a little girl, are you? But you look so sweet! Are you thirsty? Here, have some water."

It was after the dog had finished the water and was happily licking Kim's hand that she looked up.

"I see you've met Cupcake," the cutest guy she'd ever seen said. "I'm Jae."

"I'm Kim," she said. "Nice to meet you. Welcome to the neighborhood."

They'd barely started talking when Kim heard someone yelling. From the other side of the bushes, her mom shouted, "That dog's a *pit bull*, Kim. Get over here right now before that dog *bites* you! Those dogs are so *aggressive.* Come *here!*"

"Mom," Kim said calmly. *"Relax.* She's so friendly and sweet. Her name's Cupcake!"

I don't *care* what its name is. Come home *now!*

Kim looked at Jae, and then looked down at her feet, not sure of what to say next.

"Go ahead," Jae said. "We can talk later. And maybe you can show me how to get to school."

"Sure, Jae. I'd like that. And maybe we can take Cupcake for a walk."

Well, Kim thought as she returned home. *Maybe the rest of the summer won't be so boring after all.*

---

2 **Work in groups.** Discuss the questions.

1. What happens in the story?

2. What are some of the misconceptions in the story?

3. Kim's mom probably embarrassed her in front of Jae. Why are teens sometimes embarrassed by their parents? Do the parents know they're doing it? Explain.

3 **Connect ideas.** In Unit 1, you learned how people can misunderstand others and be misunderstood. In Unit 2, you learned about misunderstood animals. In both situations, people are involved. What does this tell you about the way we think? About our misconceptions?

4 **Choose an activity.**

1. Choose a topic:
   • no one understands me
   • no one understands (animal)

2. Choose a way to express yourself:
   • a short story
   • a song or a poem
   • a video

3. Present your work.

Unit 3

Everybody's Doing It!

"There is socially contagious behavior when you're in a crowd."

—Iain Couzin

A group of nearly 2,000 kayaks and canoes

1. Look at the photo. What are the people doing? Do you think they meant to do this? Explain.

2. Think about a time when you were in a large group like the one in the photo. What was going on? Why were you and all the other people there?

3. According to Iain Couzin, when we're in a group, we tend to act like the others in the group. Do you agree with him? Why or why not? Give examples.

Humans usually make their own choices about joining groups. Do you think animals can make these same choices? Discuss. Then listen and read. TR: 30

We've all looked up at the sky to see a group of birds flying together. We might see noisy geese flying in a V-shaped **formation** as they **migrate** to a warmer climate, or a spiral of starlings at sunset. Or, unfortunately, we may have seen a group of mosquitoes or wasps coming at us! On land, we might see a group of wild horses running free, or a group of dogs in a field, or a group of monkeys in trees. Underwater, we might see a group of fish swimming together in sudden but perfectly **coordinated** movement.

A group of fish swimming
away from a sailfish

Most groups that humans **belong to** have **leaders**. Sometimes, though, we may be in crowds with no leaders, as in a stadium full of sports fans. Can we **assume** that animal groups act in the same way? In the case of elephants, the oldest female is the leader. All her offspring, or young, and their offspring remain with her for many years. But in the case of fish that assemble in groups, there is no one leader. The fish come to an agreement together through **consensus**. They see what their neighbors are doing and mimic their behavior. If they see a **potential** predator, they will all quickly swim away together to avoid it. Any fish that **prefer** to go off alone are probably going to be lunch!

Scientists now **realize** that **collective** behavior in animals is a highly **efficient system** that is beneficial in many ways. These group behaviors allow animals to complete their **migrations** in relative safety, find food, and protect group members from predators.

2 **Learn new words.** Listen and repeat. TR: 31

3 **Work in pairs.** Can you think of other animals that belong to groups with leaders? Other animals that belong to groups without leaders? Make a list for each type of animal. Share your lists with the class.

Iain Couzin liked animals as a child, but it was as an adult that he decided to focus on *efficient / collective* behaviors in animals. He came to *realize / assume* that, unlike the rhino or leopard, not all animals *prefer / migrate* to live or hunt alone. He discovered that many animals have highly *potential / coordinated,* complex social *systems / consensus* that permit them to do things as a group that they could never do alone. His studies on birds, fish, and insects allow scientists to find *potential / assumed* solutions to problems such as how humans affect animal habitats, oil spills, and even world hunger.

5 **Learn new words.** Listen for these words and match them to their synonyms. Then listen and repeat. TR: 32 and 33

to assemble	crowd	to mimic	to remain

_____ 1. group

_____ 2. stay

_____ 3. imitate

_____ 4. come together

6 **Choose an activity. Work in pairs.**

1. Why do animals remain in groups? What are the advantages? Are there any disadvantages? Make two lists.

2. Some animal behaviors seem unselfish. Individual members will put the good of the group above their own. Describe an example.

3. You want to form a group at school. What are three rules that group members would have to follow? Why are those rules important?

SPEAKING STRATEGY TR: 34

Expressing cause	Expressing effect
Since <u>she's scared of wasps, we stayed indoors</u>.	<u>She's scared of wasps</u>, so <u>we stayed indoors</u>.
Because of <u>the lack of food, the animals had to travel farther and farther away</u>.	There was a lack of food. As a result, <u>the animals had to travel farther and farther away</u>.
<u>The experiment was called off</u> due to <u>the poor weather conditions</u>.	<u>The weather conditions were poor</u>. Consequently, <u>the experiment was called off</u>.

7 **Listen.** How do the speakers express cause and effect? Write the words and phrases you hear. TR: 35

8 **Read and complete the dialogue.**

Alex: Iain and his team worked with army ants, too.

Billy: What did they want to find out?

Alex: _____ ants are so social, the team wanted to see how they organize their collective behaviors.

Billy: Don't they live together in huge groups?

Alex: Yeah, and _____ , they have to be super organized.

Billy: It makes sense, I guess, _____ their numbers.

Alex: Yes, there are usually tens of thousands of ants moving at one time. _____ potential traffic jams, they organize a kind of superhighway.

Billy: And, _____ , everyone keeps moving?

Alex: Yes! The ants with food use a wide middle lane, and the ants that aren't carrying anything form lanes on the side.

9 **Work in groups.** Take turns. Use a coin to move. (Heads = 1 space; tails = 2 spaces) Express cause or effect.

10 **Work in pairs.** Humans are harming many habitats. What are some reasons for this?

Go to p. 159.

47

Two-word verbs

Separable	Inseparable
The scientists **talked over** the problem.	The scientists **talked about** the problem.
The scientists **talked** the problem **over**.	The scientists **talked about** it.
The scientists **talked** it **over**.	
	The scientists **looked into** the evidence.
They **figured out** a solution.	The scientists **looked into** it.
They **figured** a solution **out**.	
They **figured** it **out**.	

11 **Read and complete the sentences.** Make any necessary changes.

apply to	calm down	cheer up	count on
figure out	hold back	look at	turn out

Humans love to laugh. In fact, even hearing other people laugh can _____ *cheer* _____ us _____ *up* _____ or make us smile. But sometimes, even when it isn't appropriate, we just can't help ourselves and we start laughing too! Who hasn't seen people trying hard to stop giggling and to _____ themselves _____ in a place where they should be quiet?

Yawning is another common contagious behavior. When you _____ someone who's yawning, you usually want to yawn too. Can you _____ that yawn _____ ? Probably not. It's very hard to resist the urge!

Did you know that even animals yawn? It _____ that chimpanzees, dogs, lions, and other animals yawn when an animal in their group yawns.

Why are these behaviors so contagious? Scientists think they have _____ the answer _____ . They believe the same reason _____ both behaviors. They are old, basic ways to show a social connection with others in your group.

12 **Read the text in Activity 11 again.** Circle four sentences with separable verbs. Two can be rewritten without separating the verb. Write them below.

_____

_____

13 **Learn new words.** Do you think gorillas and wolves can yawn contagiously? Listen. Then listen and repeat. TR: 37 and 38

a **troop** of gorillas

a **flock** of birds

a **herd** of elephants

a **swarm** of ants

a **pack** of wolves

a **school** of fish

14 **Work in pairs.** Go back to p. 44. Take turns reading sentences in the first paragraph aloud. Each time you see the word _group_, say instead one of the words in Activity 13.

15 **Work in groups.** Listen again. Then take turns using verbs from the list to summarize the information. TR: 39

build up	carry out	clean up	rely on	respond to

16 **Work in pairs.** Talk about three surprising things you have learned about contagious behavior. Use some verbs from the list.

calm down	cheer up	figure out	respond to	think about	turn out

17 **Before you read, discuss in pairs.** The title of the reading is *Humans in Groups*. What groups do you belong to? Make a list.

18 **Learn new words.** Find these words in the reading. What do you think they mean? Use the context to help you. Then listen and repeat. TR: 40

flash mob	to influence	intention	to join	to stand out

19 **While you read, notice definitions and examples in the text.** TR: 41

20 **After you read, work in small groups to answer the questions.**

1. What is the main idea of the reading?

2. What are some kinds of groups mentioned in the reading?

3. Why do people want to join groups?

4. How are in-groups and out-groups different?

5. What are emergent groups? Have you ever belonged to an emergent group? Explain what happened.

21 **Define words.** Choose five words or phrases from the reading. Make a two-column chart. Write the word or phrase on the left, and its definition on the right.

A flash mob in Bucharest, Romania

Humans in Groups

You and all humans belong to many kinds of groups. In some, membership is involuntary—that is, you were not part of the decision to belong. For example, if you were born in Peru, you are a member of the group Peruvians. Other examples of involuntary group membership include left-handed people or brown-eyed people.

Most of the time, though, you and the rest of us want to join, or become members of, certain groups. Why? Joining the technology club, the school chorus, or a volunteer group that visits people in the hospital reflects your interests and becomes part of your social identity. You become an accepted member of the chosen in-group. At the same time, you remain different from the out-group, those people who are not in the group. This reflects the human desire to belong, but also the desire to stand out, or be seen as different.

Most groups we join have the intention of lasting over time. They work to influence others in some way. But sometimes emergent groups form without goals or structure. The members of emergent groups don't know each other, but come together suddenly to respond to an event. For instance, a group of people might see a car accident and immediately come together to help the victims.

Not all short-lived groups deal with accidents or disasters. A flash mob, which is a group of people who suddenly assemble to perform in public, only comes together for a short time and then disappears. The goal of a flash mob is to do something surprising and entertaining in public, such as having a pillow fight or dancing in the street.

Whether we're fighting with pillows or helping people, humans are social beings who come together in groups.

22 **Discuss in groups.**

1. Go back to your own list of the groups you named in Activity 17. What kinds of groups were named? Compare and contrast the groups.

2. In Unit 1, you learned about your personal identity. In this unit, you learned about your social identity as a member of groups. How do these two identities influence one another? Give an example.

3. Would you like to be in a flash mob? What would you want the flash mob to do?

VIDEO ▶

23 **Before you watch, discuss in pairs.** Compare your own abilities with those of an ant. Name something an ant can do that you cannot.

24 **Read and circle.** The video you're going to watch is called *Smarter by the Swarm*. The video is about swarm intelligence. Can you guess what that means? Circle the letter.

    a. the ability of people to pressure each other into doing something

    b. improved knowledge and ability that comes when organisms work together

    c. ants living in a colony

25 **Watch scene 3.1. While you watch, note two benefits of ants working together.**

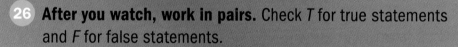

26 **After you watch, work in pairs.** Check *T* for true statements and *F* for false statements.

    1. Your brain is about 4,000 times larger than an ant's brain. Ⓣ Ⓕ

    2. Ants often look lost when they're in large groups. Ⓣ Ⓕ

    3. Ants leave a scent that sends a message to other ants in the colony. Ⓣ Ⓕ

    4. Ants can communicate the fastest route to get to a place. Ⓣ Ⓕ

    5. Companies are mimicking ant behavior to be more efficient. Ⓣ Ⓕ

    6. These companies learned that ant behavior isn't effective in humans. Ⓣ Ⓕ

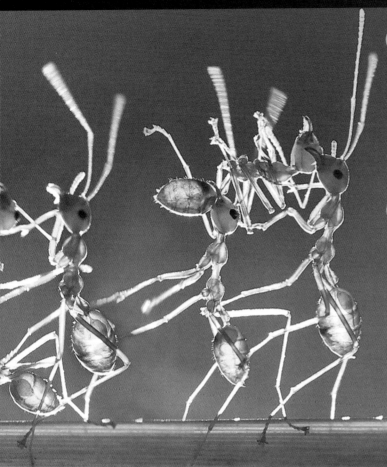

27 **Work in pairs.** What is *swarm intelligence*? Describe the meaning of this term. Use examples from ants and people in your answer. Then go back to Activity 24. Did you have the correct answer?

28 **Discuss in groups.** Think about shipping, transportation, and airlines. Why is it important for vehicles to work together? What do you think happens if a truck, boat, or plane doesn't communicate with others in its group? Compare this with what happens if an ant doesn't communicate with the rest of its colony.

A group of weaver ants work together to carry a drop of water back to their nest.

29 **Choose an activity.**

1. **Work independently.** Create a comic strip with ants as the main characters. Have your comic strip show both individual and group behavior with ants.

2. **Work in pairs.** Find out about a team of people who work together to solve problems. Explain who's on the team and what each person's role is. Share your answers with the class.

3. **Work in groups.** Imagine that you're a team of researchers and you have a group of microbots. Develop a project idea for how they can work together to get something done. Explain the goal of the project and how the microbots would make it happen.

Enough, too many, too much: Talking about amount

I have **enough** pillowcases, but there are **not enough** feathers. I need more.

You've put **too many** in each pillowcase. We've run out of feathers.

Do you want to join the flash mob pillow fight?

No way. All those people and feathers, too? It's **too much** stress for me.

30 **Listen.** For each sentence you hear, check the correct amount. TR: 43

	less than needed	the right amount	more than needed
1.	☐	☐	☐
2.	☐	☐	☐
3.	☐	☐	☐
4.	☐	☐	☐

31 **Read and complete the dialogue.**

Carlos: Do you want to join our flash mob later? Right now, we don't have

_____ people participating.

Juan: No, thanks. I have _____ things I have to do
this afternoon.

Carlos: You don't have _____ time to see Gloria? She'll
be there.

Juan: Really? Okay then, I'll do my errands afterward. They shouldn't take

_____ time.

32 **Work in groups of three.** Take turns playing *Rock, Paper, Scissors*. The winner
chooses one item from list A and one from list B. Then the winner chooses another
player to make a sentence with the chosen items. Each correct sentence is worth
1 point. The player with the most points at the end wins.

LIST A:	LIST B:
enough	dancers
not enough	money
too many	people
too much	time
	pillows

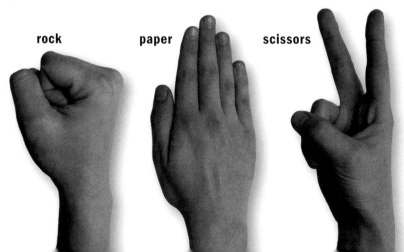

rock   paper   scissors

WRITING

In writing, using good examples is one way to explain and support the main idea. We can introduce examples with phrases such as:

for example   for instance   in other words   such as

33 **Read the model.** Work in pairs to identify the parts of the writing. How does the writer introduce examples? Underline the phrases.

Sometimes I like to be alone, but I usually prefer to be with my friends. My friends and I enjoy being together because we're interested in a lot of the same things. For instance, we all like sports, and most of us play on the school football team. We also ride our bikes to places we like, such as the park.

But our favorite thing is going to the mall on Saturdays. We like looking in the stores, but we have fun doing crazy things, too. In other words, we like to get people's attention. For example, we might all wear one blue sock and one red sock to see if anyone notices. Or we might pretend to look for a lost contact lens on the floor to see if someone else will start looking.

One time, we made up a foreign-sounding language and pretended that we were tourists from another country. We had a map and pretended to ask for directions in our fake language. But it was so funny, we couldn't stop laughing. Unfortunately, by now most people at the mall know us, so they just ignore us!

34 **Work in pairs.** What examples of group behavior does the writer describe? Are any of them contagious group behavior? If so, which ones?

35 **Write.** Choose a human group behavior or an animal group behavior. Write a description of this behavior. Be sure to include several examples.

Collaborate

"From invasive cells to schooling fish to human cultures, groups can accomplish what solitary individuals cannot."

—Iain Couzin
National Geographic Explorer, Behavioral Ecologist

1. Watch scene 3.2.

2. Iain studies group behavior of birds, insects, fish, and other animals. What other group behaviors could we learn from?

3. When is it better to work alone? To work in a group? Name something that you accomplished as a group member that you couldn't have done alone.

Make an Impact

A **Plan and carry out a flash mob activity.**

· Choose an activity to carry out as a flash mob.

· Notify people on social media about the time and place
  of your flash mob.

· Film your flash mob and present it to the class.

B **Plan and make a video of human group behavior.**

· With a group, go to a crowded place. Pretend to look for
  something on the floor, such as a contact lens.

· One group member should film what happens for two or three
  minutes. Take notes on any contagious behavior.

· Write the results of your experiment, and present them to
  the class.

C **Plan and carry out a photo shoot in nature.**

· Choose a local insect or bird to observe.

· Research its group behaviors and take photos.

· Write and present a report to the class.

"When you buy a piece of clothing, there should be a personal connection."
—Asher Jay

Fashion Footprints

Boys in São Paolo, Brazil

1. Are these boys dressed the same? Discuss the similarities and differences.

2. Do you choose the clothes you wear? Why do you wear the clothes you do?

3. Do you have a personal connection with all of the clothes you wear? Why or why not?

1 **Why do people wear the clothes they wear?**
Discuss. Then listen and read. TR: 44

There are many different reasons we buy and wear the clothes we do. We choose clothes for practical reasons, such as weather and comfort. We also wear the clothes we do for psychological reasons. These include wanting to feel powerful, to feel attractive, and to show our **creativity** and personality. Wearing certain **styles** affects how we feel about ourselves and how other people see us. We may care about the latest **trendy** fashion by popular **designers**, or we may prefer practical clothes.

And finally we make our clothing choices for social reasons, such as showing we want to **fit in** with a group, or making a statement about our beliefs.

The environment is another reason that clothing choice is important. The clothes we buy and wear **have an impact** on the planet. This is known as our fashion **footprint**. Each one of us has our own individual footprint. We need to **take responsibility for** our clothing decisions and **do our part** to reduce our fashion footprints.

These Japanese teens show off their accessories in Harajuku Square.

60

crop

cotton

Cotton uses more pesticides than any **crop** in the world.

A lot of our clothing is made from natural **materials** such as **cotton**, wool, leather, and silk. **Synthetic** materials, such as nylon and polyester, are also very popular. But all of these materials, whether natural or synthetic, affect the environment. For example, many **toxic** **chemicals** are used to make leather shoes. The **manufacture** of cotton jeans requires enormous amounts of water and energy. And if dyes are used to color any of these materials, then even more water, energy, and toxic chemicals are required.

2 **Learn new words.** Listen and repeat. TR: 45

3 **Work in pairs.** Talk about what's in your closet. Describe the materials your clothes are made of. What is your favorite outfit? How often do you wear it?

4 **Read and write the words from the list.** Make any necessary changes.

cotton	creativity	designer	fit in
manufacture	style	take responsibility for	trendy

Asher Jay has a great sense of _____ , but she also cares about our planet. She's a fashion _____ , or a person who designs clothes. She's also an artist, writer, and environmental activist. Asher wants us all to _____ protecting the environment and animals. In one fashion line, she created _____ shirts, dresses, and skirts influenced by the bright oranges and greens of endangered coral reefs. For Asher, fashion is more than an effort to _____ with a crowd. She believes the clothes you wear can communicate both a message you care about and your own _____ .

5 **Learn new words.** Listen for these words and match them to the definitions. Then listen and repeat. TR: 46 and 47

attractive	popular	psychological	social

_____ 1. mental

_____ 2. having a quality that people like

_____ 3. related to people being
   with one another

_____ 4. liked by many people

6 **Choose an activity. Work in pairs.**

1. Some schools require students to wear uniforms. What social or psychological reasons might they have for doing this?

2. Discuss. Do you dress more for yourself or for the impression you might make on others? Do you and your friends dress in a similar way? Is it better to fit in or to stand out? Why?

3. Do a video interview. Ask your classmates about their favorite outfits and why they like them.

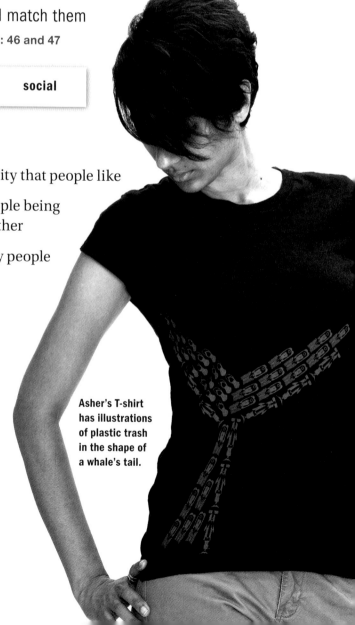

Asher's T-shirt has illustrations of plastic trash in the shape of a whale's tail.

Asking for clarification	Clarifying
When you say _____ , what do you mean?	What I meant was _____ .
Are you saying that _____ ?	That's right./No, that's not it. I meant _____ .
Could you explain that a little more?	Sure. I was referring to _____ .

7 **Listen.** How do the speakers make sure they're communicating clearly? Write the phrases you hear. **TR: 49**

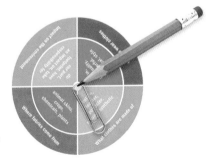

8 **Read and complete the dialogue.**

Pat: I like to choose my clothes depending on my mood.

Ken: When you say "mood," _____?

Pat: I _____ whether I feel happy, nervous, sad—whatever.

Ken: Oh. _____?

Pat: _____ my feelings. When I feel really happy, I like to wear bright colors like yellow, red, and orange. When I'm sad, I wear black or gray. And when I'm nervous, I wear my favorite old blue sweater—especially on test days.

Ken: _____ it's your lucky sweater?

Pat: Yes, I guess so. It makes me feel calmer.

9 **Work in groups.** Spin the wheel and discuss, using the words for each topic as instructed. Ask for clarification and clarify as needed.

Go to p. 155.

10 **Work in pairs.** How does asking for clarification and clarifying help you communicate? How can it help other people, such as doctors or teachers, communicate?

GRAMMAR TR: 50

Present passive: Describing actions and processes

They use a lot of pesticides to grow cotton.

They make a lot of clothing from synthetic materials.

A lot of pesticides **are used** to grow cotton.

A lot of clothing **is made** from synthetic materials.

11 **Listen.** Circle all the passive forms you hear. TR: 51

are bought	are made	are required	are used	is made	is used

12 **Read.** Underline all examples of the present passive voice.

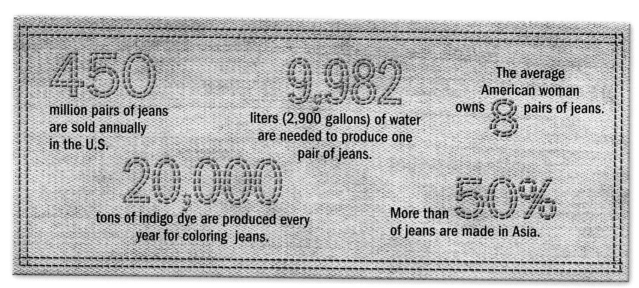

450 million pairs of jeans are sold annually in the U.S.

9,982 liters (2,900 gallons) of water are needed to produce one pair of jeans.

The average American woman owns 8 pairs of jeans.

20,000 tons of indigo dye are produced every year for coloring jeans.

More than 50% of jeans are made in Asia.

13 **Work in pairs.** Talk about how jeans are made. Change the verbs to the present passive.

1. People make jeans with a material called denim.

2. They make denim out of cotton.

3. They sometimes mix polyester or other synthetic materials into the denim.

4. They dye the denim yarn before they make the denim fabric.

5. After they cut the fabric and make the jeans, they prewash them.

6. They sometimes add stones when they prewash jeans to make them look older.

> Jeans are made with a material called denim.

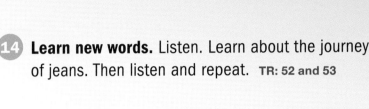

14 **Learn new words.** Listen. Learn about the journey of jeans. Then listen and repeat. **TR: 52 and 53**

to ship

to assemble

factory

warehouse

retail store

to purchase

15 **Work in pairs.** Look at the infographic above. Use the present passive to describe the journey of jeans. Use the words in the box to describe the process.

after that	finally	first	then

16 **Work in groups.** Use the present passive to describe how something else is done or made.

17 **Before you read, discuss in pairs.** Based on the title and the photos, what do you think the reading is about?

18 **Learn new words.** Find these words in the reading. What do you think they mean? Use a dictionary to check. Pay attention to the pronunciation of each word. Then listen and repeat. TR: 54

to donate	eco-friendly	entrepreneur
to give back	profit	

19 **While you read, look for similarities and differences.** TR: 55

Santana Draper

20 **After you read, work in pairs to answer the questions.**

1. What's the main point of the reading?
2. What's unusual about the two designers?
3. How did Santana Draper and Maya Penn get their start?
4. What's one important reason they were successful?
5. How do the two designers use part of their profits?

21 **Compare and contrast Maya and Santana.** Use a Venn diagram to organize information.

22 **Discuss in pairs.**

1. What do you have a passion for—music? art? sports? animals? Why?

2. Santana and Maya are following their passion and finding success. Do you think it's better to follow your passion or to do something more practical?

3. Imagine you create a company and earn a lot of money. Would you use any of your profits to help people? To help the environment? Why or why not?

A Passion for FASHION

Pursuing a dream isn't just for grown-ups. These young designers grew up with a passion for fashion—and for helping others.

Santana Draper is a young entrepreneur with a giving spirit. When he was very young, he overheard adults discussing a terrible storm. The storm affected families and left their children without holiday presents. Santana offered to give his toys away as gifts for the children. He said that he could make more toys for himself out of paper. The name of his company today? PaperToy Clothing!

Santana's parents supported his creativity, and decided to have some of his sketches printed on T-shirts. People who saw Santana's work wanted to know where they could purchase the T-shirts, and an online fashion business was born. He designs T-shirts for males from 10 to 25 years old, and has created a "wear and give" program to give back to his community. For each T-shirt a customer buys, part of the sale price goes toward a program to feed hungry children. "I want to inspire boys and young men to action by producing wearable art that lives with you," Santana says.

Teenage entrepreneur Maya Penn was only eight years old when she started her first business, Maya's Ideas. She makes eco-friendly clothing and accessories that are sold in many countries, including Australia, Canada, Denmark, and Italy. When Maya was very young, her mother taught her to sew. Maya would find pieces of fabric around the house to turn into a scarf or hat. When she wore her creations in public, people would stop her and ask where they could buy them!

Even before she opened her business, Maya knew she wanted her clothes to reflect her beliefs. She decided that her items had to be eco-friendly, and that she would donate 10 to 20 percent of her profits to charities and environmental organizations. "I've had a passion for protecting the environment and its creatures since I was little," Maya says.

Maya Penn

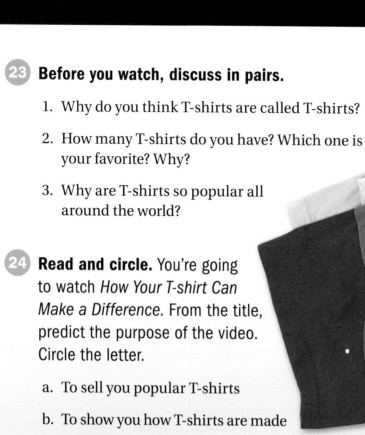

23 **Before you watch, discuss in pairs.**

1. Why do you think T-shirts are called T-shirts?

2. How many T-shirts do you have? Which one is your favorite? Why?

3. Why are T-shirts so popular all around the world?

24 **Read and circle.** You're going to watch *How Your T-shirt Can Make a Difference*. From the title, predict the purpose of the video. Circle the letter.

a. To sell you popular T-shirts

b. To show you how T-shirts are made

c. To help you make good choices

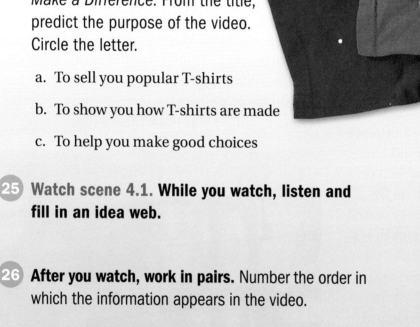

25 Watch scene 4.1. **While you watch, listen and fill in an idea web.**

26 **After you watch, work in pairs.** Number the order in which the information appears in the video.

_____ T-shirts use a lot of water and energy.

___1___ Cotton is everywhere.

_____ There is a solution. We can make a difference!

_____ We don't have as much water on the planet as we think.

_____ Cotton has a major impact on the planet.

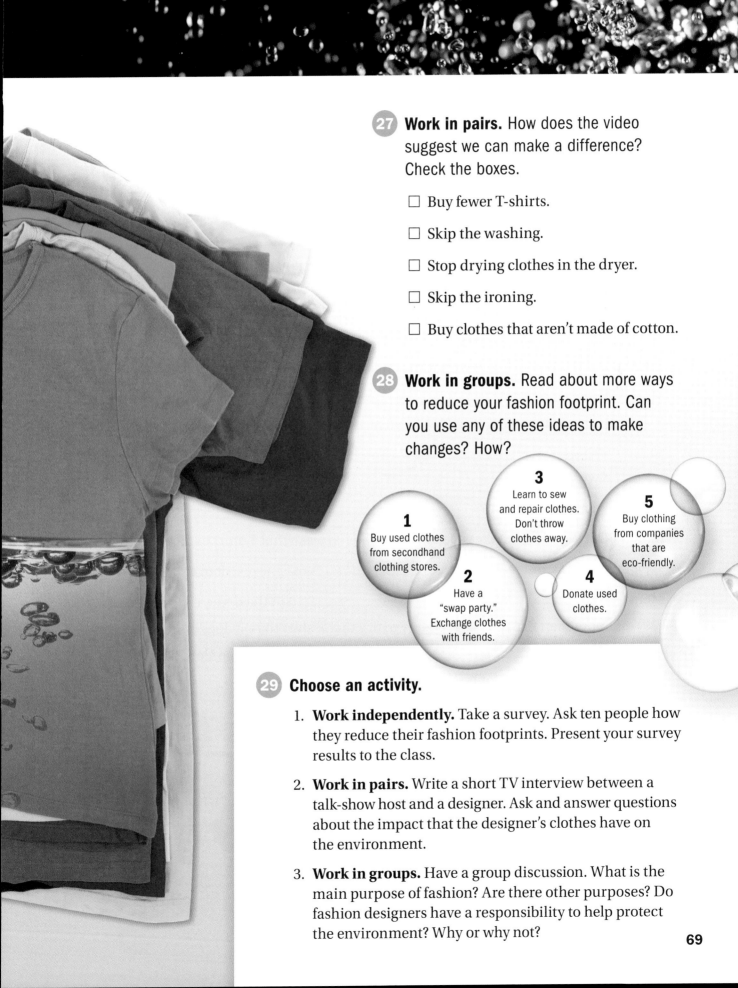

27 **Work in pairs.** How does the video suggest we can make a difference? Check the boxes.

☐ Buy fewer T-shirts.

☐ Skip the washing.

☐ Stop drying clothes in the dryer.

☐ Skip the ironing.

☐ Buy clothes that aren't made of cotton.

28 **Work in groups.** Read about more ways to reduce your fashion footprint. Can you use any of these ideas to make changes? How?

1 Buy used clothes from secondhand clothing stores.

2 Have a "swap party." Exchange clothes with friends.

3 Learn to sew and repair clothes. Don't throw clothes away.

4 Donate used clothes.

5 Buy clothing from companies that are eco-friendly.

29 **Choose an activity.**

1. **Work independently.** Take a survey. Ask ten people how they reduce their fashion footprints. Present your survey results to the class.

2. **Work in pairs.** Write a short TV interview between a talk-show host and a designer. Ask and answer questions about the impact that the designer's clothes have on the environment.

3. **Work in groups.** Have a group discussion. What is the main purpose of fashion? Are there other purposes? Do fashion designers have a responsibility to help protect the environment? Why or why not?

30 **Read.** Complete the dialogue with words from the list. Use *could*, *should*, *could have*, or *should have*.

| be | do | dry | hang | listen | put | wash | wear |

Mom: You ____shouldn't have washed____ your new T-shirt. You just got it!

Pat: But I wore it to lunch with my friends, and I spilled soup on it.

Mom: You _____ more careful. And instead of washing your T-shirt all by itself in the machine, you _____ it by hand in the sink. That way you save water.

Pat: What do you mean?

Mom: Did you know it takes 40 gallons of water to wash that T-shirt in the machine?

Pat: That much? I really _____ it in there.

Mom: And you _____ it in the dryer, either. It takes more than five times the energy to dry that T-shirt than it does to wash it. From now on, you _____ it on the clothesline so that the sun dries it—for free!

31 **Work in pairs.** Take turns tossing a coin. (Heads = 1 space; tails = 2 spaces) Make suggestions and give advice about present and past actions as instructed.

Go to p. 161.

WRITING

In persuasive writing, we can support our point of view with facts and statistics. We use phrases such as:

_____ states that

according to _____

the facts show that _____

research shows that _____

32 **Read the model.** Work in pairs to identify the parts of the writing. How does the writer persuade the reader? Underline the phrases.

Have you ever seen someone wearing fur? Some people think fur is a fashion statement. Other people think it is more important to stop killing animals.

Research shows that millions of animals are killed for their fur each year. Some are hunted and trapped in the wild. Even more die at what are called fur-factory farms. According to groups that protect animals, most of the skins that people buy come from fur farms. On these farms, animals live in small, dirty cages until it's their turn to die.

People in the fur business say they help control animal populations. But the facts show that animals control their own populations. Fur factories also claim they do not have an impact on the environment, but that's not true, either. A real fur coat takes more than 20 times the energy needed to make a fake fur coat! The chemicals fur factories use also pollute the water.

Fashion lovers should know that every fur coat, jacket, vest, or hat represents animal suffering. This harm to animals and the environment will end only when people do their part and stop buying and wearing fur.

A mink

33 **Work in pairs.** Does the writing persuade you to do something about wearing fur? Why or why not?

34 **Write.** Persuade your readers to reduce their fashion footprint.

Make Good Choices

**"I believe in a hands-on approach.
Today we need everyone's involvement."**

—Asher Jay

National Geographic Explorer, Creative Conservationist

1. **Watch scene 4.2.**

2. What are some things you can do by yourself or in your community to help protect animals used for fashion? To protect other animals?

3. What good choices can you make in your everyday life to protect the environment? Give at least three examples.

Make an Impact

A **Plan and write a blog entry about reducing one's fashion footprint.**

· Write the text.

· Collect photos and drawings.

· Share the blog and respond to questions and comments.

B **Plan and hold an eco-friendly fashion show.**

· Collect donated and found materials.

· Use the materials to design clothing and accessories.

· Have a fashion show and film it.

C **Plan and hold a Fashion Footprint Awareness Day.**

· Make posters and brochures.

· Conduct interviews in the community.

· Report on the day's activities for the school newspaper.

Express Yourself

The Garb Age

Fashion is about excess,
about wanting more.
It's indulgent, vain,
selfish to the core.

Excess is euphemism
for avoidable waste.
Buying without need
is in poor taste.

In a finite world
resources are scarce.
Surplus drains, and
Earth has no spares.

Fads repeat like history,
dated becomes news.
Reduce, repurpose, recycle.
Up-cycle and reuse!

Fight a failing model.
Save scraps, set the stage.
Sew your own designs,
but don't let your garb age.

② **Work in groups.** Discuss the poem.

1. What do you think the poem is
   about? Circle the letter. Support
   your answer.

   a. buying trendy fashions
   b. reducing your fashion footprint
   c. buying only recycled clothing

2. The poem says we shouldn't buy
   things we don't need. Do you agree
   or disagree? Explain.

3 **Connect ideas.** In Unit 3, you learned about group behaviors. In this unit, you learned about fashion trends. What connection do you see between the two topics?

4 **Choose an activity.**

1. Choose a topic:
   • fashion and group behavior
   • clothing and its impact on the environment

2. Choose a way to express yourself:
   • a poem or rap
   • a poster
   • a short video

3. Present your work.

75

1. We all know that birds fly. What other living things fly? Make a list of as many as you can.

2. Why do you think humans have always wanted to fly?

3. Would you like to be able to fly? Why or why not?

Jetmen flying over the city of Dubai, United Arab Emirates

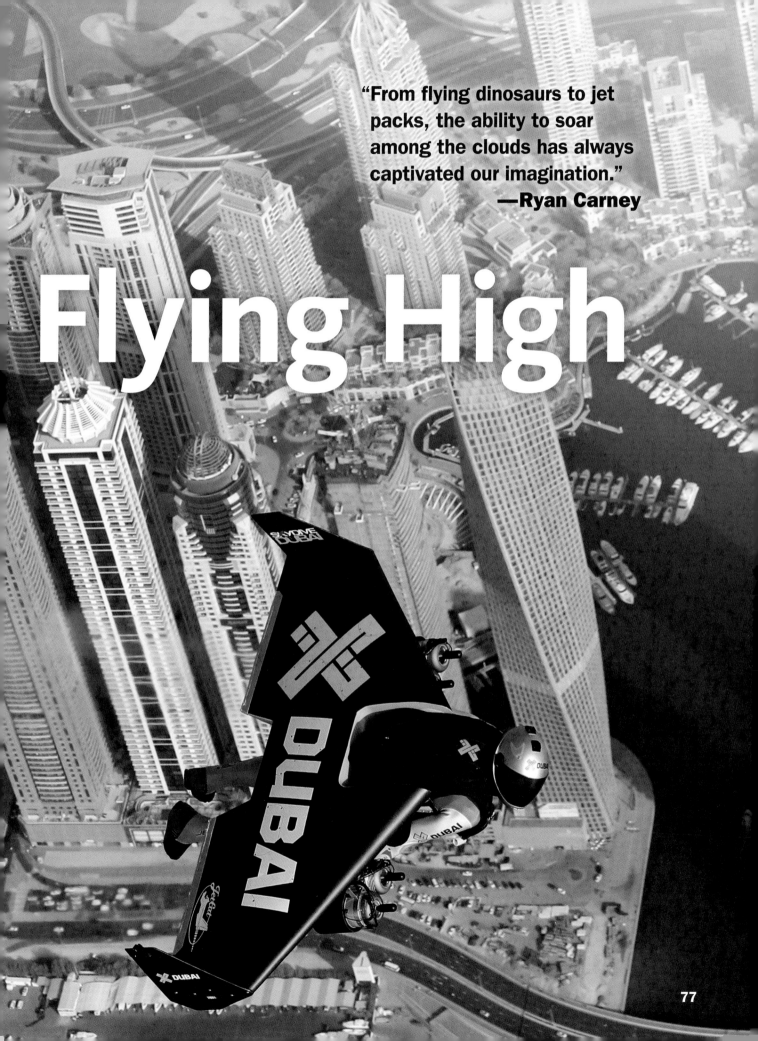

"From flying dinosaurs to jet packs, the ability to soar among the clouds has always captivated our imagination."
—Ryan Carney

Flying High

350 million years ago

Today it's hard to imagine an empty sky, but many millions of years ago, there was no **flight** of any kind. All life was **limited** to water or land. This included very **early** insects, which were the first animals to develop wings around 350 million years ago. How did wings **evolve**? The most accepted theory is that wings developed from structures that originally supported insects' ancestors as they moved in the water. Over time, these structures became larger and stronger. They turned into wings that first allowed insects to jump and then **glide**. Eventually, insects were able to **flap** their wings and fly.

229 million years ago

By 229 million years ago, flight had also developed in pterosaurs, large flying reptiles. These animals were not dinosaurs, but were closely related to them. They were good fliers because they had strong flight muscles, skin-covered wings, and strong but **hollow** bones. They could glide, flap their wings, and even **soar**, using the wind to help them stay in the air. The largest flying animal ever was a pterosaur named *Quetzalcoatlus*, which had a head as big as a human and a body as tall as a giraffe. *Quetzalcoatlus* had a **weight** of 200 kg (440 lb.) and a **wingspan** of 11 m (36 ft.)!

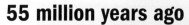

150 million years ago

Today's birds are actually living dinosaurs! The earliest known dinosaur that is generally considered to be the first bird is *Archaeopteryx*. It had feathered wings like modern birds, but also shared **features** with reptiles, such as teeth, clawed fingers, and a bony tail. It could fly, but not very well. Later birds became more skilled fliers due to better flight **adaptations**.

55 million years ago

The fourth and last appearance of flight happened 55 million years ago, when the ancestors of bats developed the **capability** of powered flight. It's likely that these mammals lived in trees and first became gliders. Over time, their bodies formed wings, making bats the only mammals that have evolved to fly.

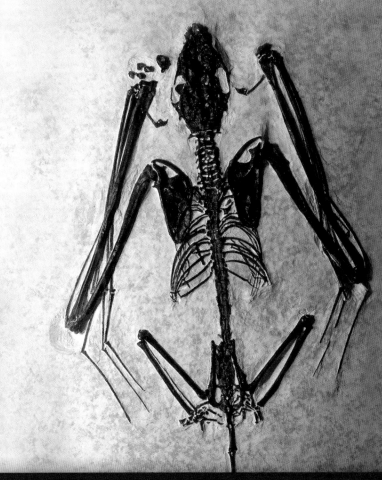

2 **Learn new words.** Listen and repeat. TR: 59

3 **Work in pairs.** The capability of flight has evolved in four groups: insects, pterosaurs, birds, and bats. Why do you think each of these animals evolved to fly? How did it benefit them? Do you imagine any other animals evolving this way in the future? Explain.

4 Read and write the words from the list. Make any necessary changes.

adaptation	capability	evolve	flight
glide	hollow	limited	weight

Archaeopteryx **feather fossil**

As an evolutionary biologist and paleontologist, Ryan Carney studies the history of dinosaurs and their modern-day descendants—birds. From a single feather, he was inspired to research the _____ that species made over time in order to fly. He is interested in *Archaeopteryx* because it was the earliest known dinosaur. Archaeopteryx was also the earliest species to _____ the _____ of powered flight. Ryan investigates the theory that _____ in birds originated from "the ground up" (from ancestors that first ran on the ground), and not from "the trees down" (from ancestors who lived in trees and then learned to _____ , before eventually flying).

Ryan Carney

5 Learn new words. Listen for these words and match them to their definitions. Then listen and repeat. TR: 60 and 61

to allow	powered	skilled	to support

_____ 1. provide the capability to do something

_____ 2. having the capability to do something

_____ 3. help someone or something do something

_____ 4. having energy to produce movement

6 Choose an activity. Work in pairs.

1. List three insects that fly and three that don't. Compare the insects on the two lists. What are the advantages of flying for insects?

2. With around 10,000 species in existence, birds have developed a wide variety of adaptations for flight. Compare and contrast two very different-looking birds. How is their flight similar? How is it different?

3. Why do you think bats developed flight to use mainly at night? How are bats' flight adaptations different from those of other fliers?

SPEAKING STRATEGY TR: 62

Arguing	Conceding
I'm sure you agree that _____ .	I guess you have a point.
Well, I think that _____ .	
Most people support _____ .	Well, maybe you're right.
Yes, but what about _____ ?	

A colugo

7 **Listen.** How do the speakers argue their points and concede? Write the phrases you hear. TR: 63

8 **Read and complete the dialogue.**

Ann: You know, we still don't know much about the ancestors of bats. There just isn't much evidence.

Alan: Maybe, but _____ the idea that bats are closely related to a group of mammals that also includes the colugo.

Ann: Yes, _____ the fact that the colugo glides? It doesn't flap its wings and fly.

Alan: Well, I _____ bats and colugos probably had an ancestor in common at some point. Think about it. I'm

_____ that they share characteristics. Their wings look very similar. And both species eat insects. So it's logical that their ancestor would be a nocturnal glider who lived in trees.

Ann: I _____ there.

9 **Work in groups.** Cut out the cards. Take turns reading them aloud. Group members argue and concede each point.

> All birds that fly have wings, but not all birds that have wings fly.
>
> Argue YES or NO.

Go to p. 163.

10 **Work in pairs.** What affects your own life? What do you want to change? Take turns arguing and conceding.

> Most students support the idea of less homework. I do, too.

> Yes, but what about preparing for tests? Homework can be useful for that.

> Well, maybe you're right.

Past perfect: Talking about the first of two actions in the past

Pterosaurs disappeared. Humans evolved.	Pterosaurs **had** already **disappeared** by the time humans evolved.
The capability of flight developed four times in animals. Humans tried to fly.	By the time humans tried to fly, the capability of flight **had developed** in four groups of animals.

11 **Listen.** Which of the two actions in the past happened first? Check the box. TR: 65

1. ☐ kite flight ☑ animal flight
2. ☐ running, arm flapping ☐ kite flight
3. ☐ measuring, signaling ☐ human transport
4. ☐ fun and entertainment ☐ military use
5. ☐ kites made of paper ☐ kites made of silk

12 **Read and complete the sentences.** Use past perfect forms of the verbs in the box.

design	draw	forget	jump	try

Jumping from towers, walls, and cliffs was among many ways humans tried to fly. Many men _____ to fly like the birds before success was achieved in 875 CE. In that year, a man named Abdul Qasim Abbas Ibn Firnas jumped from a high wall built over a valley in Cordoba, Spain. Before his experiment, he _____ wings covered in feathers. He planned to wear them on his arms and legs. He also _____ on paper a series of wing movements to use in flight. According to the people who saw his experiment, he began to fall after he _____ . Afterward, he climbed even higher than his starting point. He glided for several hundred feet, turned, and came back to the wall. He hurt his back in the experiment, possibly because he _____ to include a tail in his design.

1000 BCE
The Chinese invent kites.

875
Abbas Ibn Firnas wants to **prove** that man can fly. He tries flying by jumping with feathered wings.

1295
Marco Polo describes man-carrying kites.

13 **Learn new words.** Listen. Learn about Leonardo da Vinci and the history of human flight. Then listen and repeat. **TR: 66 and 67**

14 **Read the sentences.** Check T for *true* or F for *false*.

1. Gravity is one of the forces that acts on flying and falling objects. Ⓣ Ⓕ
2. Leonardo da Vinci designed his parachute in 1595. Ⓣ Ⓕ
3. A stable flying object does not move from side to side. Ⓣ Ⓕ
4. Da Vinci created a helicopter that ascended into the sky at an angle. Ⓣ Ⓕ
5. A parachute can be used to help people descend safely from the sky. Ⓣ Ⓕ
6. Experts proved that da Vinci's glider was almost the same as Cayley's. Ⓣ Ⓕ

15 **Work in groups.** Use the timeline and new words to make four true sentences about flight. Use the past perfect.

1. _____
   _____

2. _____
   _____

3. _____
   _____

4. _____
   _____

1485
Leonardo da Vinci studies **forces** that affect objects in the air in order to design flying machines.

1595
Fausto Veranzio designs a **parachute**.

1670
Francesco Lana de Terzi designs an airship.

1783
The Montgolfier brothers launch hot air balloons. These balloons **ascend** when the air inside is hot and **descend** when it cools.

1800
George Cayley designs the first **stable** glider to carry a human.

16 **Before you read, discuss in pairs.** What do you know about the Wright brothers and flight? Make a list. What are three facts you expect to find in the reading?

17 **Learn new words.** Find the words in the reading. What do you think they mean? Then find the words *land*, *fuel*, and *pilot* in a dictionary. Look at the different ways these words can be used. Then listen and repeat all of the new words. **TR: 68**

| engine | fuel | to land | pilot | to take off |

18 **While you read, notice the order in which events happened.** **TR: 69**

Reaching
FOR THE Sky

The Dream of Human Flight

One day while traveling, Milton Wright saw a small toy helicopter that was powered by rubber bands. He bought this toy for his two young sons, Orville and Wilbur. Mr. Wright surely had no idea this simple act would lead to the creation of the world's first powered airplane. The toy gave the brothers a strong interest in flight. They soon began trying to build similar models themselves.

When they were older, the Wright brothers decided they wanted to make a "small contribution" to the field of flight. At that time, most attention on flight focused on hot air balloons and gliders. However, the brothers were more interested in a heavier flying machine, powered by an engine and controlled by a pilot. They first read all the books they could on the early mechanics of flight. Then they used kites to better understand the forces that controlled objects in the air.

Over the next three years, the Wright brothers worked on designs and shapes for different types of gliders. During this time, they worked with engineers Otto Lilienthal and Octave Chanute, both authors of books on flight. These men were important influences on the brothers' work.

In December, 1903, Orville Wright takes off with his brother Wilbur running beside him.

The brothers had built a wind tunnel to test different shapes of wings and tails for their gliders. Then they began to think about how to get a flying machine weighing 272 kg (600 lb.) into the air and keep it there. They designed a 12-horsepower engine that generated enough force to allow the Flyer to take off from the ground in December 1903. It ascended about 3 m (10 ft.) into the air, and continued to fly 36 m (120 ft.) in about 12 seconds. The first heavier-than-air flight became a reality!

The second, third, and fourth flights followed on the same day. But the Wright brothers observed that the Flyer was not stable enough and was hard to control. They spent two more years perfecting their airplane. Finally, on October 5, 1905, Flyer III flew about 39 km (24 mi.) in 39 minutes. The plane landed only because it ran out of fuel. The dream of human flight had finally come true.

1891

Otto Lilienthal builds a glider.

1894

Octave Chanute's book on flying machines is published.

1891

Samuel Langley creates his aerodrome model.

1901

Alberto Santos-Dumont circles the Eiffel Tower.

1905

The Wright brothers fly for 39 minutes in Flyer III.

19 **After you read, work in pairs to answer the questions.**

1. What is the main idea of the reading?

2. How did the Wright brothers prepare for their project?

3. Whose ideas on flight influenced the Wright brothers?

4. The Wright brothers worked on their flight project for years. What personality characteristics do you think they had that helped them reach their goals?

20 **Put the events in order.**

_____ The Wright brothers built a wind tunnel to test the wings and tails of their gliders.

_____ They read everything they could about flight.

_____ They flew Flyer III about 39 km (24 mi.) before it ran out of fuel.

_____ They designed a 12-horsepower engine to power the Flyer.

__1__ They used kites to learn more about how things fly.

_____ They worked for two years to make the Flyer more stable.

21 **Discuss in groups.**

1. How do you think the Wright brothers' work helped shape the twentieth century? What aspects of life changed?

2. Is just one person ever truly responsible for a great idea or invention? Do all ideas and inventions build on the work of previous generations? What do you think? Why?

VIDEO ▷

22 **Before you watch, discuss in pairs.** What makes bees different from other insects? Why are bees important?

23 **Work in pairs.** You're going to watch a video called *Flight of the RoboBee*. Based on the title and the photo, predict what the video is about.

24 Watch scene 5.1. **While you watch, list three benefits that robotic bees will have.**

1. _____
2. _____
3. _____

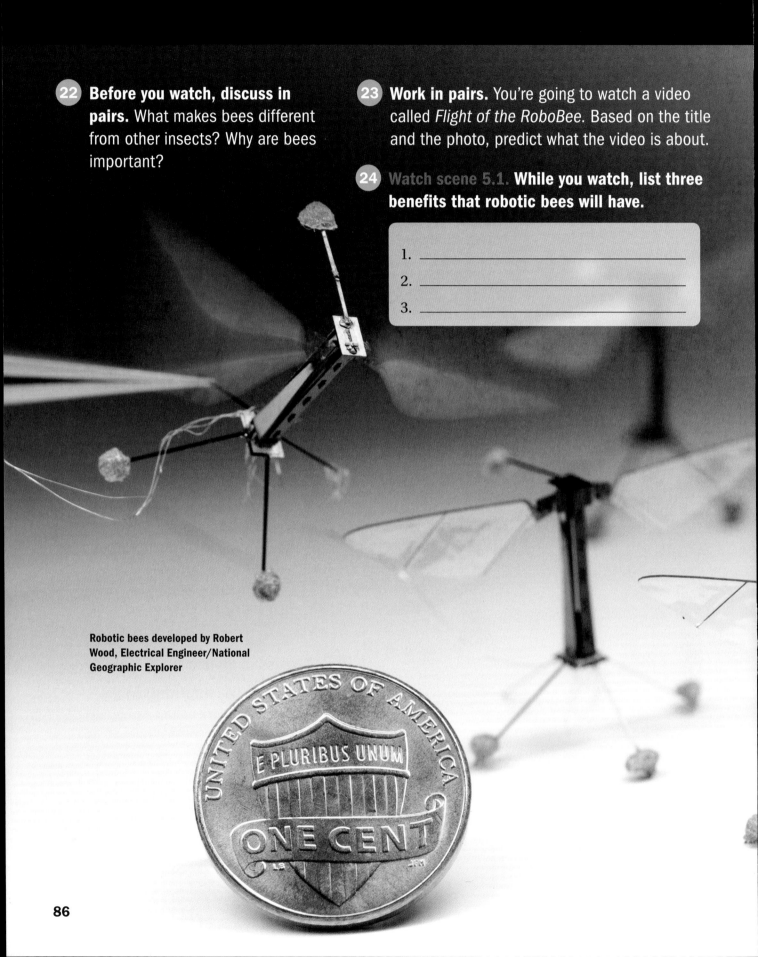

Robotic bees developed by Robert Wood, Electrical Engineer/National Geographic Explorer

25 **After you watch, work in pairs to decide if each sentence is *true* or *false*.** Check the correct answer.

1. Robert Wood says that most new robots are large, powerful, and dangerous.   (T) (F)

2. Robert's robots are inspired by nature.   (T) (F)

3. Robert looks at real insects to figure out how to construct his robotic bees.   (T) (F)

4. Robotic bees don't have the supports necessary to fly independently.   (T) (F)

5. Robert doesn't plan to send robotic bees into dangerous areas because they could break.   (T) (F)

6. Getting the robots to fly was a long, difficult process for Robert and his team.   (T) (F)

26 **Discuss in groups.** In the video, Robert says, "If you don't fail, you don't learn enough." Explain what you think he means by this.

27 **Work in groups.** You learned about man's early attempts at flying. Compare and contrast the process of getting the robotic bee to fly with the processes of the flight pioneers you learned about.

28 **Choose an activity.**

1. **Work independently.** Research other robotic insects that are being developed. Choose one and create a short presentation on it. Explain what it's used for. Compare it with the robotic bee.

2. **Work in pairs.** Robert says that robotics is "the next big thing to impact our lives." Find an example of a robot that is making an impact on people's lives. Write an article about this robot and the impact it's having.

3. **Work in groups.** Create a poster to advertise robotic bees. Use illustrations and text to describe them, and explain why they are useful.

GRAMMAR TR: 70

Past perfect progressive: Talking about the first of two actions in the past

The Wright brothers **had been working** on powered flight for several years before Wilbur Wright flew for 2 hours and 19 minutes in 1908.

Before Louis Bleriot first crossed the English Channel in an airplane in 1909, pilots **had been using** hot air balloons.

---

29 **Read.** Complete the sentences with past perfect progressive forms of the verbs in parentheses.

1. Otto Lilienthal _____ (use) gliders for around five years before he crashed in one in 1896.

2. Before Samuel Langley's large Aerodrome A crashed while taking off, he _____ (build) smaller machines that flew successfully.

3. Before Alberto Santos-Dumont made the first successful powered flight in Europe, he _____ (win) awards for his flights in balloons.

4. Engineer Frank Whittle _____ (work) on his theories for nine years before he tested his first jet engine in 1937.

5. Before Charles Yeager became the first pilot to travel faster than the speed of sound in 1947, he _____ (fly) for about five years.

Charles Yeager

30 **Work in pairs.** Take turns tossing the cube. Ask and answer questions. Use the past perfect progressive.

Before you became part of the (group/team), how long _____ you _____ ?

Before modern airplanes appeared, how long _____ inventors _____ ?

Before you started this class, how long _____ you _____ ?

> Before you became part of the team, how long had you been playing basketball?

> I had been playing basketball for six years.

Go to p. 165.

88

When we classify, we organize our ideas into categories. First we introduce the topic. Then we divide it into categories. Each category gets its own paragraph in the essay. In each paragraph, we describe shared characteristics that make up that category. A classification essay ends with a conclusion. In the conclusion, we bring the categories back together to talk about the main topic.

31 **Read the model.** Work in pairs to identify the categories and details.

Long before we had airplanes, people had been experimenting with different flying machines. We still use some of those flying machines today. Some depend on air for movement, while others use engines.

Hot air balloons and gliders use air currents for movement. Hot air balloon pilots steer their aircraft by ascending or descending into air currents that move the balloon. The pilot controls the balloon's movement by heating the air inside the balloon, or by allowing it to cool naturally.

A glider also uses air currents to soar and glide. Small planes pull gliders along a runway to help them take off. But once in the air, gliders use the currents, not an engine, to move. Their long wingspan and strong body give riders a safe, smooth flight. Hot air balloons and gliders are most often used for fun and adventure.

Helicopters first appeared during World War II. A helicopter doesn't have wings, but, like an airplane, it has an engine that makes its blades spin at high speeds. This allows the helicopter to ascend into the sky. Unlike an airplane, which has to keep moving, helicopters can stay in one place in the sky for a long time. Today helicopters are mostly used by medical teams and the military. But you can also take a helicopter ride for fun. Many tourist destinations offer helicopter rides for sightseeing.

So before your next airplane ride, remember that airplanes aren't the only way to fly.

32 **Work in pairs.** What does the writer classify? How many categories are there? What details are mentioned in each part?

33 **Write.** Write a classification essay to describe two types of animal flight.

Explore Your Interests

"As an evolutionary biologist, I get to combine both childhood interests into my research: dinosaurs and animation!"

—Ryan Carney

National Geographic Explorer, Paleontologist/Evolutionary Biologist

1. **Watch scene 5.2.**

2. What are your interests? How have they changed over the years? Is there anything that you were interested in as a child that you are still learning about? What is it?

3. The people you read about in this unit, from Leonardo da Vinci to Ryan Carney, made their interests their life's work. How could you turn your own interests into a career? What would you need to do?

Make an Impact

Ⓐ Design a flying machine.

· Plan and design a flying machine.

· Use your plans to create a model of the machine.

· Present your machine to the class. Explain how it works.

Ⓑ Make an evolution poster.

· Choose an animal that has evolved the capability of flight.

· Research how this animal has evolved over time. Draw and label at least four steps in its evolution.

· Arrange your drawings in order on a poster. Display the poster in class.

Ⓒ Advertise a flying machine.

· Choose a flying machine that you learned about.

· Think about the benefits and risks of using that machine.

· Make an advertisement for the machine. Try to persuade your audience to fly in it.

A pilot guiding a homemade machine during a flying competition in Moscow, Russia

New Frontiers

"We are pushing the frontiers in our own solar system, sending missions to other worlds, looking outward to distant pinpoints of light."
—**Bethany Ehlmann**

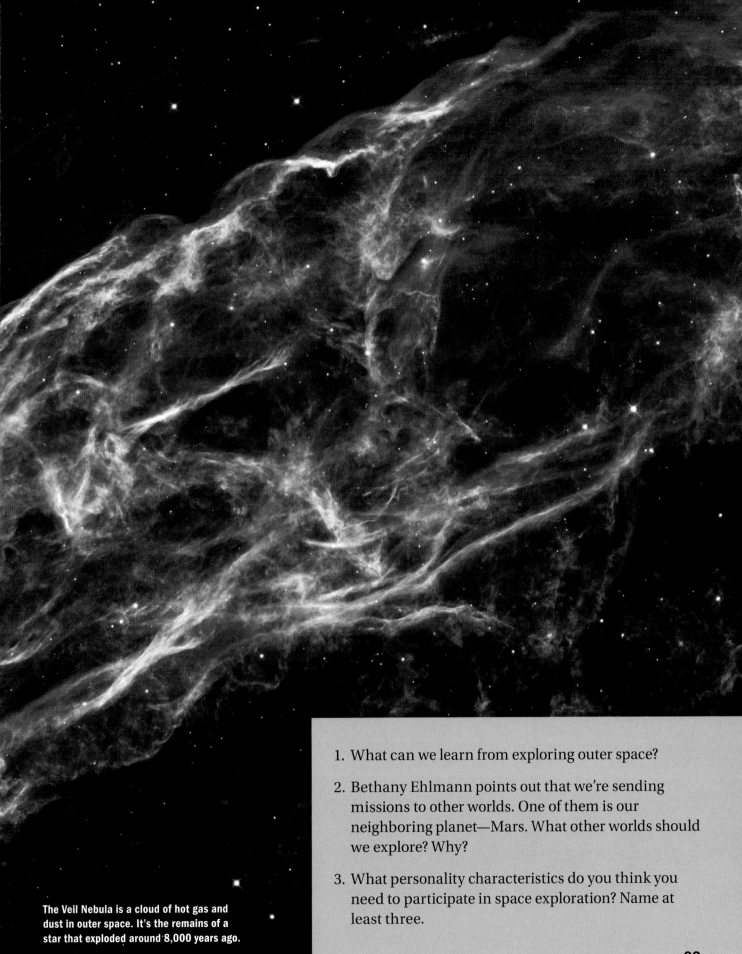

The Veil Nebula is a cloud of hot gas and dust in outer space. It's the remains of a star that exploded around 8,000 years ago.

1. What can we learn from exploring outer space?

2. Bethany Ehlmann points out that we're sending missions to other worlds. One of them is our neighboring planet—Mars. What other worlds should we explore? Why?

3. What personality characteristics do you think you need to participate in space exploration? Name at least three.

1 **Recent space exploration has focused on Mars. Why do you think this is?**
Discuss. Then listen and read. TR: 71

We think of Earth as the *Blue Planet* and Mars as the *Red Planet* when looking at **satellite** images of them. Although they look very different, our home planet and Mars are actually similar in many **aspects**. Like Earth, Mars has its own **atmosphere** and clouds. Both planets have large, ice-covered areas called *polar caps*. Mars's **landscape** includes features also found on Earth, such as mountains, **plains**, channels, craters, and even volcanoes.

Both planets have days that are about 24 hours long, and both spin on an invisible line called an *axis*. Each planet tilts to the side on its axis, at an angle of about 24 **degrees** in relation to the sun. This tilt is what causes the seasons to change on both planets.

The Curiosity rover on the surface of Mars

Astronomers have always **wondered** if life exists beyond Earth. If it does, our neighbor Mars is the most likely place to find it. Mars is a planet of wild extremes. It has the largest **dust** storms, the deepest and longest **valley**, the highest mountain, and the largest volcano known in our solar system! But to most planetary scientists, the biggest question is whether life is, or was, possible on the planet.

Advances in technology have allowed scientists to equip robots with a variety of tools, and then send them to explore Mars. These scientific **instruments** have been able to **detect** real **proof** that life is possible there. For example, one of the **fundamental** requirements for life, the existence of some form of water, has been discovered in several areas of Mars. A **vast** amount of ice is under the surface and also frozen in the polar caps year-round. In 2015, scientists confirmed that liquid water exists on Mars's surface. But will this finding **lead to** the discovery of life on the Red Planet? We're still waiting to find out.

Channels on Mars's surface suggest the presence of water.

2 **Learn new words.** Listen and repeat.
TR: 72

3 **Work in pairs.** Why is it important that scientists find proof of water on Mars? Do you think that they will find life on the Red Planet? Why or why not?

95

4 **Read and circle the correct word.**

As a planetary geologist, Bethany Ehlmann studies our solar system. She *wonders / leads to* how the rocks on Mars were formed and how they interacted with water. She also is looking for *degrees / proof* that life could have been or could be present on the Red Planet. She works closely with Curiosity, a six-wheeled robot called a *rover*. Rovers can move around and explore. Curiosity travels through the plains and *valleys / aspects* on the surface of Mars. It uses scientific *dust / instruments* to analyze the Martian *proof / landscape.* Bethany hopes that Curiosity's work, combined with new technological advances, will one day provide the answer to the *fundamental / satellite* question: Is there life beyond Earth?

5 **Learn new words.** Listen to these words and match them to the definitions. Then listen and repeat. TR: 73 and 74

advance	astronomer	to equip with	requirement

_____ 1. provide

_____ 2. progress, technology

_____ 3. something that's necessary

_____ 4. a person who studies the stars and planets

Bethany Ehlmann with a Mars rover

6 **Choose an activity.**

1. **Work independently.** Go online to learn more about the Curiosity rover's mission. Write a paragraph about what you learned.

2. **Work in pairs.** Make a Venn diagram. Compare and contrast Earth and Mars.

3. **Work in groups.** Hundreds of years ago, adventurers spent years exploring countries and continents, leaving everything they knew behind them. If you knew you would spend years away, and maybe never return, would you explore Mars? Why or why not? Discuss with your group. Then share with the class.

SPEAKING STRATEGY TR: 75

Speculating

Do you think that <u>they'll ever find life on Mars</u>?

Most likely, <u>scientists will research the topic for a long time</u>.

I'll bet <u>they're close to finding life</u>!

It's likely that <u>they'll first find microbes</u>.

What if <u>scientists really do find evidence of life</u>?

I'm pretty sure that <u>will change everything</u>!

7 **Listen.** How do the speakers speculate? Write the phrases you hear. TR: 76

8 **Read and complete the dialogue.**

Mia: I just read a really interesting article about the Curiosity rover on Mars. By examining the soil, it helped scientists learn more about ancient Mars.

Lee: Well, _____ they had to dig really deep to find soil and rocks from ancient times.

Mia: That's not true. The article said that 50 percent of the rock on Mars's surface is from ancient times.

Lee: So _____ that scientists can really learn much from studying some old rocks?

Mia: Well, yes. _____ these rocks hold information about the possibility of life on Mars. The samples that Curiosity collected show that the chemicals needed to support life were present on the planet.

Lee: _____ Curiosity discovers living creatures on Mars?

Mia: _____ we won't see photos of little green Martians, if that's what you mean. _____ if Curiosity can find proof of life, it will be microscopic organisms found in the icy regions.

9 **Work in pairs.** Take a card and look at the photo from Mars. Speculate about what you see. Your partner will read the correct information. Then switch roles.

> What if this is food growing on Mars? I'll bet they'll try sending some back to Earth.

> Actually they're mineral balls found on Mars's surface. I'm pretty sure that we won't want to eat them!

10 **Work in groups.** Speculate about the near future. How well are you going to do on your next test? How well is your favorite sports team going to do this year? How soon are you going to make a new good friend?

Round balls of minerals found on Mars

Go to p. 167.

GRAMMAR TR: 77

Present and past conditionals: Talking about unlikely (but possible) or impossible situations

Unlikely but possible

If I **were** a scientist, I **would focus** my research on Saturn.

He **would be** a space tourist if he **had** the money.

Impossible

If I **had known** about the talk on Mars, I **would have gone**.

They **could have fixed** the rover if they **had equipped** it **with** better tools.

Habitable by Humans?

The planet Saturn is made up of gas, so it doesn't have a **habitable** environment. If scientists wanted to find life around Saturn, they would have better luck studying two of its moons: Enceladus and Titan.

11 **Listen.** What's the reality in each case? Check the box. TR: 78

1. ☐ I'm not president.   ☐ I'm president.
2. ☐ The project succeeded.   ☐ The project failed.
3. ☐ I investigated Titan.   ☐ I didn't investigate Titan.
4. ☐ There is one space station. ☐ There are two space stations.
5. ☐ We repeated the experiment. ☐ We didn't repeat the experiment.
6. ☐ I don't explore space.   ☐ I explore space.

12 **Read.** Complete the sentences with the correct form of the verbs in parentheses.

Saturn has always been a fascinating planet. At about 1.2 billion km (746 million mi.) from Earth, it was the most distant of the worlds recognized by ancient sky watchers. If they _____ (study) it the way we are able to today, they _____ (be) amazed. They _____ (find) that its rings consisted of billions of icy particles. They _____ (discover) that these rings are extremely thin—only 10 m (33 ft.) thick. And they _____ (learn) that some of the planet's small moons play an important part in controlling the orbits and spacing of the rings. If you _____ (study) Saturn's moons today, you _____ (observe) that some of its 62 moons orbit in opposite directions. You _____ (see) that some moons even exchange orbits. Most importantly, you _____ (learn) that two of the moons have the potential for life!

13 **Learn new words.** Look and listen. Learn about Saturn's moons Titan and Enceladus. Then listen and repeat. TR: 79 and 80

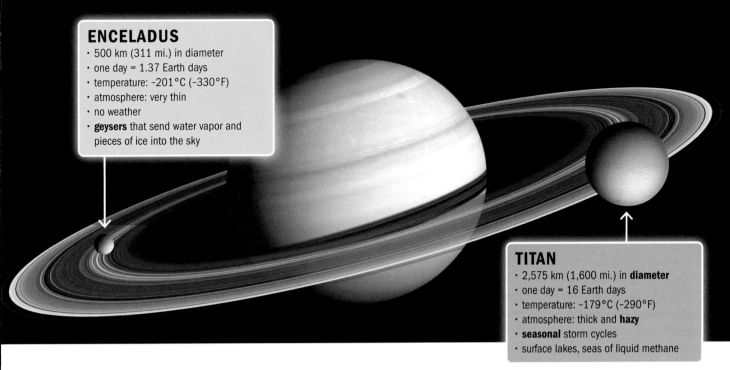

ENCELADUS
· 500 km (311 mi.) in diameter
· one day = 1.37 Earth days
· temperature: -201°C (-330°F)
· atmosphere: very thin
· no weather
· **geysers** that send water vapor and pieces of ice into the sky

TITAN
· 2,575 km (1,600 mi.) in **diameter**
· one day = 16 Earth days
· temperature: -179°C (-290°F)
· atmosphere: thick and **hazy**
· **seasonal** storm cycles
· surface lakes, seas of liquid methane

14 **Work independently.** Imagine you spent a year living on Titan and are now back home on Earth, talking about it with a friend. Complete the sentences with present or past conditionals.

1. If you _____ (have) the right equipment, you _____ (visit) Titan and be able to experience life on a moon.

2. If you _____ (come) to Titan while I was there, would you _____ (swim) with me in a surface lake?

3. If I _____ (know) you would be living on Titan, I _____ (remind) you about the seasonal storm cycles.

4. If I _____ (be) on Titan today, I _____ (try) to take photographs of the storms.

5. If Enceladus _____ (be) habitable by humans, I _____ (go) there next year.

6. If I _____ (go) to Enceladus, I _____ (study) the geysers.

15 **Work in groups.** If you had to visit one of these two moons, which one would you choose? Why? Give two or three reasons.

> If I could travel to one of Saturn's moons, I'd go to Enceladus to see the geysers.

More Than a Dream

16 **Before you read, discuss in pairs.** When we think of space, we think of astronauts. But there are many other types of jobs in any space mission. Other than astronaut, what other kinds of space-related jobs can you think of?

17 **Learn new words.** Find these words in the reading. What do you think they mean? Think about the parts of each word. Use a dictionary to check. Then listen and repeat. TR: 81

aspiring	background	chance
leadership	perseverance	

18 **While you read, think about the different categories that the information can be organized into.** TR: 82

19 **After you read, work in pairs to answer the questions.**

1. What is the main purpose of the reading?

2. Who is Alyssa Carson? Why is she mentioned in the reading?

3. What do you think happens at a space camp session?

4. Besides camp, what can aspiring astronauts do to prepare for space?

Astronauts-in-training testing a surface transport vehicle in the desert

Could space be your own new frontier?

Are you one of Earth's next generation of explorer-astronauts? What do aspiring astronauts do to prepare for the possibility of a career in space?

A good person to ask would be Alyssa Carson. Her dream is to be the first person on Mars. As a child, Alyssa read as much as possible about Mars, studied its maps, and did everything she could to learn about the Red Planet. This included going to a space-themed camp for the first time at age seven. Since then, Alyssa has attended more than 20 such camps. In fact, at age 13 she was the first person ever to complete all the NASA Space Camps in the world. At these camps, future astronauts get the chance to ride in space-flight simulators and experience what zero gravity feels like.

While Space Camp may not be possible for everyone, there are many other ways to prepare for a future in space. If you're interested, consider the following:

- Astronauts must be in excellent physical condition. Now's the time to begin a healthy lifestyle of a balanced diet, regular exercise, and plenty of sleep.

- Astronauts need to meet a wide range of physical challenges. Skills acquired through activities such as scuba diving, skydiving, skiing, mountain climbing, and piloting aircraft are extremely valuable. Now's a great time to start learning these types of skills little by little.

- Astronauts need to meet a wide range of emotional challenges. Work on developing positive traits, such as patience, cooperation, and perseverance. Take every opportunity to practice team-building, leadership, and problem-solving skills.

- Astronauts need to have a strong background in math and science. Work with your school's counselors and mentors to determine the best courses to take. Keep up with real-time developments and discoveries in space.

- Don't forget languages! In addition to English, you'll need to know other languages such as Russian and Chinese to communicate successfully.

Alyssa Carson

20 **Work in pairs.** Classify the types of challenges astronauts face. Give examples of each type.

21 **Discuss in groups.**

1. Of the challenges astronauts face, which do you think are the hardest? Why?

2. Alyssa Carson is preparing for her dream career as an astronaut. What's your dream career? What can you do now to prepare for it?

3. One day humans may live in space colonies. What would an ordinary family's typical day be like in a space colony? Would you like to live in a space colony? Why or why not?

VIDE⯈

22 **Before you watch, discuss in pairs.** You've learned about the possibility of life beyond Earth. What are three characteristics of places where life is considered to be possible?

23 **Read and circle.** The video you're going to watch is called *Europa: Ocean World.* Based on what you've learned in this unit, predict what the video will be about. Circle the correct letter.

   a. another world with an ocean

   b. an ocean near Europe

   c. a new world discovered by Europeans

24 Watch scene 6.1. **While you watch, think about the requirements for life.** Circle the ones you hear mentioned in the video.

warm temperatures	energy
liquid water	plants
gases	substances found in rocks

25 **After you watch, work in pairs.** Circle the correct answer.

   1. Kevin Hand says that life on Earth may have begun in our *oceans / caves.*

   2. Where you find liquid *lava / water,* you generally find life.

   3. Europa's ocean has existed for *ten thousand / billions of* years.

   4. *Earth / Europa* has more water and deeper oceans.

   5. Scientists used to think that for a world to be habitable, it had to be *the right distance from / in orbit around* the sun.

   6. Now scientists realize that life is possible wherever there are the key elements for life: water, energy, and the building blocks found in *plants / rocks.*

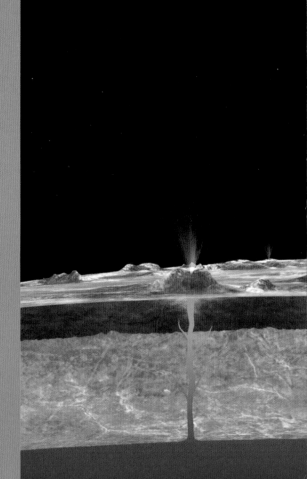

This illustration shows what scientists believe is a global liquid ocean under Europa's surface. Jupiter (right) and another of its 67 moons, Io, are in the background.

26 **Work in pairs.** You've learned about three moons so far in this unit. Compare and contrast Europa with Titan and Enceladus. How are they the same? How are they different? Create a diagram to show your ideas.

27 **Work in groups.** To answer the question of whether there is life in Europa's oceans, scientists must collect information from those oceans. Name two challenges scientists face in gathering that information.

28 **Choose an activity.**

1. **Work independently.** Learn more about Europa. Use the information you collect to design and label a model of Europa. Present it to the class.

2. **Work in pairs.** Imagine that life has just been discovered on Europa. Write and illustrate a newspaper article explaining how that happened and what was found.

3. **Work in groups.** Imagine you work for a research group that studies Europa, and you're trying to get people to support your work. Prepare and give a presentation explaining why it's important to study Europa. Persuade your audience to support your work.

Adverbs: Comparing how things are done

The new satellite transmits data **efficiently**.

The last satellite didn't transmit data **as efficiently as** the new satellite.

The new satellite transmits data **more efficiently than** the last satellite.

The new satellite transmits data **the most efficiently** of all the satellites.

The new rover travels **fast**.

The last rover didn't travel **as fast as** the new rover.

The new rover travels **faster than** the last rover.

The new rover travels **the fastest** of all the rovers.

29 **Complete the sentences.** Use the correct forms of the adverbs in parentheses.

Astronomers had dreamed of a telescope that would photograph the universe

_____ (clearly) than telescopes on the ground could. That

dream came true in 1990 when the Hubble Space Telescope was launched into orbit

_____ (approximately) 612 km (380 mi.) above the Earth.

Hubble has photographed some of _____ (spectacularly)

beautiful images of space ever taken. But that's not all. It has _____

(greatly) expanded our knowledge of space. Before Hubble astronomers could not estimate

the age of the universe _____ (precisely) they can now. Because

of what they've seen through Hubble, astronomers have estimated that the universe is

around 14 billion years old.

What's after Hubble? The Webb Space Telescope, which will measure distant objects

even _____ (accurately) than Hubble.

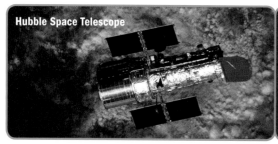
Hubble Space Telescope

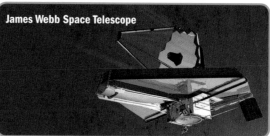
James Webb Space Telescope

30 **Work in groups.** Spin each wheel. Take turns comparing how group members do or have done different activities using the words from each spinner.

I have been speaking English as long as you.

Yes, but Camille has been speaking English the longest!

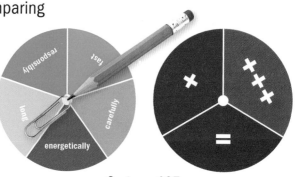

Go to p. 165.

One way to organize persuasive writing is to present both sides of an argument, point by point. First describe one argument, and then present a counterargument in the same paragraph. Do the same for additional arguments, presenting counterarguments each time.

31 **Read the model.** Work in pairs to circle one side of the argument and underline the counterargument. Do this for each point.

It's extremely important to develop new technology wisely, so that everyone can benefit from it. Some people believe our technology plan should focus on building spacecraft. Others believe it should focus on building robots. Which is the better course of action?

For those who dream of exploring outer space, the development of high-tech spacecraft is essential. But just one spaceship costs billions of dollars more to build than even the most complex robot. Many specialized robots could be designed and built much more cheaply than spaceships, and they could be used for practical purposes right here on Earth.

Many of the people who focus on future space exploration describe solving key mysteries of space and perhaps even the origin of life in the universe. While this kind of knowledge is fascinating, there are no practical benefits from it for people on Earth right now. Robots will have new applications in the future, but even the robots we currently have benefit us in practical ways. For example, they can work in dangerous conditions, such as places with extreme temperatures. They can take apart bombs, build products, or perform complex surgery—all useful things that benefit people right now.

To sum up, it's clearly better to give attention, time, and money to the technological development of robots. They are less expensive to develop and more useful. Robots also benefit people in ways that are more practical than any benefit from a spacecraft.

32 **Work in pairs.** In your opinion, which of the two positions on technological development is more persuasive? Why?

33 **Write.** Write about the argument that it's better to explore the ocean than outer space. Present both sides of the argument and persuade your readers to agree with you.

A flying robot that may be used for security, rescue, and even space exploration

Discover the Future

"Technology development is a huge part of our exploration and our ability to access the stories and the discoveries on other worlds."

—Bethany Ehlmann
National Geographic Explorer, Planetary Geologist

1. **Watch scene 6.2.**

2. Bethany uses technology to explore Mars without being there. Where else can you explore using only technology?

3. Do you believe that people will live on Mars in the future? Why or why not? What would be the advantages and disadvantages of creating a colony there?

Make an Impact

A **Design and write a postcard from outer space.**

· Research one of the places mentioned in this unit to learn more about it.

· Imagine you took a week-long journey to this place. Write a postcard message about your trip. Include information on traveling to and from your destination.

· Find a photo of the place. Create your postcard by pasting your photo on one side and your message on the other.

B **Plan a space mission.**

· Choose a place in outer space that you would like to explore.

· Design a space mission to explore that place. Write about what you would need and what you would want to find out about.

· Give a speech to the class presenting your idea. Persuade your listeners to support your mission.

C **Create an outer-space TV sitcom.**

· Write a script for a TV sitcom whose characters live in outer space.

· Work in groups to rehearse the script.

· Film your sitcom and share it with the class.

Express Yourself

1 **Read and listen to a scene from a movie script about a team of space explorers.** TR: 84

FADE IN:
EXTERIOR SPACESHIP IN ORBIT AROUND MARS

FADE TO:
INTERIOR SPACESHIP MAIN CONTROL ROOM - NIGHT

MARK and SONIA, with flashlights on, come through the doors and stop in front of a bank of dimly lit active computer screens.

                    MARK
        OK, we're here alone. Now show me
            what you're talking about.

                    SONIA
           Look at screen seventeen.
         Something strange is going on.

                    MARK
         I don't see anything unusual.

                    SONIA
           Look at the top right corner.

Mark catches his breath as he leans in to examine the top right corner of the computer screen.

                    MARK
        (turning to look wildly at Sonia)
              That's impossible!

                    SONIA
           I know. But it's there.

MARK
I can't believe it! We need to wake up
the mission commander right now.

Sonia puts her hand firmly on Mark's shoulder.

SONIA
Don't panic. We need to think.

MARK
Are you kidding?
What's there to think about?

Sonia takes a deep breath. Then she looks directly
into Mark's eyes.

SONIA
Mark, I don't trust him.

2 **Work in groups.** In this scene, two astronauts see something very unusual on their screen. What do you think they see? List three possibilities. Then compare your ideas with those of another group. Are your ideas similar? Which idea is the most surprising?

3 **Connect ideas.** In Unit 5, you learned about the history of flight. In Unit 6, you learned about space exploration. How did the early pioneers of flight set the stage for space exploration? Discuss the evolution of flight that led to spacecraft.

4 **Choose an activity.**

1. Choose a topic:
   - flight
   - space exploration

2. Choose a way to express yourself:
   - the next scene of the movie script
   - a presentation on flight (including spacecraft)
   - an original movie or play

3. Present your work.

Visual Stories

"Photography and filmmaking are very powerful ways to give people other ideas and other things to think about."
—Ami Vitale

1. The title of this unit is *Visual Stories*. Look at the photograph. What story does it tell?

2. Photographer Ami Vitale uses photography to give people new ideas and new things to think about. Should this be the goal of all photographers? Why or why not?

3. In addition to photography and filmmaking, what other kinds of visual arts tell stories?

A museum worker moves *La Bella Principessa*, which many believe was painted by Leonardo da Vinci.

Stories have been a **meaningful** form of communication throughout human history. Do you remember a time when a family member told you a story without reading it from a book? **Oral** stories are a part of every culture, and they allow us to pass traditions and values from one generation to the next. **Visual** stories have also been told in a variety of ways for thousands of years. Researchers have found rocks that were decorated by humans more than 100,000 years ago. Although the rocks had only simple linear patterns, the patterns had meaning. And it's meaning that creates a story.

People began painting on cave walls around 40,000 years ago. As time went on, painted **images** appeared on everything from pottery to **canvas**. Painting is a fairly permanent way to **represent** information. Because painted walls and objects have lasted for thousands of years, they give us a window into the past. Through this window we can see the stories of ancient Egyptians on the walls of their tombs. We can also see **scenes** from Renaissance Europe, showing the lives of people from kings to commoners. These paintings allow us to be **witnesses** to history.

In the early nineteenth century, French artist Louis-Jacques-Mande Daguerre introduced a device that provided another way to tell visual stories: the *daguerreotype*. This early camera was first used to take **portraits**. Photography with other subjects eventually became popular, but it took a while. At first people were afraid of a camera's ability to capture real life!

Today photographers like Ami Vitale use photos to **portray** how people live. Ami presents her photos in ways that create certain responses from her **audience**, such as **anger** or **shock**. "Photography creates change," she says. Ami hopes that by telling her **subjects**' stories visually, she'll get people to realize that we're more alike than we are different. This will create a greater **understanding** among people around the world.

Visual stories are told on the walls of the tomb of Queen Hatshepsut, Egypt.

2 **Learn new words.** Listen and repeat.
TR: 86

3 **Work in pairs.** Do you have a favorite painting? A favorite photograph? Describe one, and the story it tells, to your partner.

4 **Read and write the words from the list.** Make any necessary changes.

anger	audience	meaningful	portrait	portray
scene	subject	understanding	visual	witness

Ami Vitale is known for the way she _____ international news and culture in her photos. Ami worries that some people may not have a good _____ of one another's cultures, so she creates _____ stories to make us think about how we see others. She believes that photographs can make us _____ to things that we wouldn't see otherwise. Photos can show people and places in a _____ new way. Ami wants her _____ to look closely at her powerful photos and feel more connected to their _____, even if they then feel emotions like _____ or sadness.

Ami Vitale

5 **Learn new words.** Listen for these words and match them to their definitions. Then listen and repeat. TR: 87 and 88

to capture	certain	to last	permanent

_____ 1. show an idea

_____ 2. particular, specific

_____ 3. never ends or goes away

_____ 4. exist over time

6 **Choose an activity.**

1. **Work independently.** Research cave paintings or images from Egyptian tombs. Choose a selection and write a paragraph to describe the story it tells.

2. **Work in pairs.** Bring a photo from home that you feel tells a clear story. Ask your partner to tell the story he/she sees in your photo. Then tell your partner the real story.

3. **Work in groups.** Who are some well-known painters in your country? Do their paintings tell stories? If so, what stories do they tell? Discuss.

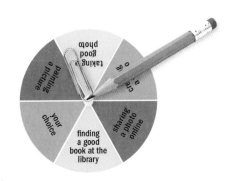

SPEAKING STRATEGY TR: 89

Explaining a process

First, <u>you need to find a good camera</u>.

The next step is <u>choosing a good location</u>.

Right after that, <u>you need to pack the right equipment</u>.

Next, <u>check the weather</u>!

Meanwhile, <u>check to see that you have enough space on your computer</u>.

Make sure to <u>save your photos when you're done</u>.

7 **Listen.** How does the speaker explain the process of sharing photos? Write the phrases you hear. **TR: 90**

8 **Read and complete the dialogue.**

Aki: Hi, Uncle Moto. I see you have your new phone. Do you have any selfies on it?

Uncle Motohiro: Selfies? What are those?

Aki: Seriously? They're photos you take of yourself on your phone.

Uncle Motohiro: What? How do you do that?

Aki: _____ , you have to open the camera app on your phone. _____ is to press the little button with the arrows on it. That will turn the camera on you.

Uncle Motohiro: OK, then what?

Aki: It's selfie time! Stretch your arm out in front of you as far as you can. _____ point the lens at your face. Hold your face at an angle—it's more interesting that way. _____ , hit the button to take your photo!

Uncle Motohiro: Ugh! It's terrible!

Aki: Ha! That's what the delete button is for!

9 **Work in pairs.** Take turns spinning the wheel and explaining processes.

10 **Work in groups.** Think of three things you typically do in a week that can be explained as processes, such as making your lunch or getting ready for school. Explain these processes. Do your group members do these things in the same ways?

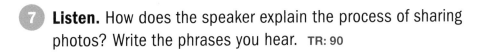

Go to p. 169.

115

Past passive: Describing past actions and processes

Goya created many of his works at night, by the light of a hat that had candles on it.

Many of Goya's works **were created** at night, by the light of a hat that had candles on it.

Painters explored many different styles.

Many different styles **were explored** by painters.

Artists usually made paint by mixing colors with oils.

Paint **was** usually **made** by mixing colors with oils.

11 **Listen.** Learn about portraits and the stories they tell. Then circle the verbs that you hear used in the past passive. TR: 92

ask	capture	create	die	display	do	invent
make	pay	require	spend	take	use	work

12 **Work in pairs.** Use the words to ask and answer questions in the past passive.

> Who painted the *Mona Lisa*?

> The *Mona Lisa* was painted by Leonardo da Vinci.

1. *Mona Lisa* / paint / da Vinci
2. Flyer III / build / Wright brothers
3. early camera / invent / Daguerre
4. cave paintings / create / early humans

Mona Lisa (La Gioconda)
by Leonardo da Vinci

13 **Work in pairs.** Look at *Portrait of a Young Woman*. Then answer questions using the past passive.

1. Who painted the portrait? _____

_____

2. What was worn by the subject? _____

_____

3. What do you think the subject was asked to do by the painter?

_____

_____

Portrait of a Young Woman
by Jean-Étienne Liotard

14 **Learn new words.** Listen to learn more about painting. Then listen and repeat.
TR: 93 and 94

A **landscape** painting shows a scene from nature.

Although their subjects are often simple, still-life paintings can be **masterpieces**.

Some portraits aren't **realistic**. They're **abstract**.

15 **Discuss in groups.**

1. Do you prefer realistic or abstract paintings? Why?

2. Can landscapes and still-life paintings be abstract? Why or why not?

3. Discuss two works of art you consider masterpieces.

16 **Work independently.** Use the past passive to describe how you think one of the works of art on these pages was created. Write at least four sentences.

_____

_____

_____

_____

BRINGING STORIES TO LIFE

Do you love playing video games with really cool graphics? Or watching action movies with amazing special effects? Thanks to advances in digital technology, modern animation can create detailed, lifelike images that move around the screen at incredible speeds. We experience animation in so many different forms, from the cartoons on our TVs to the emojis on our smartphones. But animation is nothing new. In fact, people have been trying to bring images to life for hundreds of years.

The earliest animation began in the seventeenth century with a device called the magic lantern. In the nineteenth century, other devices were developed that created movement when viewers spun them. By the turn of the

1650s

The magic lantern uses the light of a candle and painted pieces of glass to create moving images projected onto a wall. It becomes more sophisticated over time.

1832

The *phenakistoscope* is considered by many to have created the first true animation. To watch the animation, the viewer holds up a mirror and spins two illustrated disks. The spinning motion makes the illustrations seem to move.

1834

The *zoetrope* also uses a spinning motion to create animation. It quickly becomes more popular than the phenakistoscope because more than one person can watch at a time.

1891

American inventor Thomas Edison creates the *kinetoscope*. Viewers must look into the machine to watch a cartoon, which lasts about 13 seconds and contains around 50 images.

17 **Before you read, discuss in pairs.**

Which animated TV shows and movies did you watch as a child?

18 **Learn new words.** Find these words in the reading. What do you think they mean? Use a thesaurus to find synonyms for each word. Then listen and repeat. TR: 95

animation	cartoon	illustrator
method	sophisticated	

19 **While you read, underline each of the different methods of animation mentioned in the text.** TR: 96

HOW ANIMATION HAS CHANGED OVER THE YEARS

twentieth century, artists around the world were developing short animated films using hand-drawn animation. Illustrators would create thousands of drawings for a single cartoon!

Throughout the twentieth century, animators continued to develop different methods, from drawings to using clay figures. By the 1980s, digital animation was being developed. It quickly replaced traditional methods because it allowed cartoons to be produced in less time and with less money. Today advanced digital animation methods aren't just used in cartoons and video games, but also to create special effects in live-action films. Animation has become so sophisticated that sometimes we can't distinguish it from reality!

1917

Argentine animator Quirino Cristiani creates the first animated film, *El Apóstol*. The film has 58,000 illustrations and is 70 minutes long.

1928

Mickey Mouse is born. Walt Disney changes animation forever by adding sound. *Steamboat Willie* was the first cartoon in which viewers could hear what was happening.

1980s–present

Digital animation is first developed in the 1980s. Today sophisticated 3D animation is used for cartoons, video games, and even live-action movies.

20 **After you read, work in pairs to answer the questions.**

1. How was animation created with a magic lantern?
2. Name two differences between a phenakistoscope and a zoetrope.
3. How many drawings did Quirino Cristiani use to create the first animated movie? How long was it?
4. How did Walt Disney's *Steamboat Willie* cartoon change animation?
5. Why did digital animation replace traditional methods?
6. What are two ways that 3D animation is used today?

21 **Work in pairs.** Compare the words and phrases you underlined with your partner. Then summarize how each method was used to tell a visual story.

22 **Discuss in groups.**

1. If you had to animate a story, which method would you choose? Why?
2. Go online to watch *Steamboat Willie*. Describe the cartoon in your own words. Compare it with cartoons that children watch today.

VIDEO ▶

23 **Before you watch, discuss in pairs.** In the reading, you learned that most modern animation is digital. How do you think digital animation is made? Describe the process.

24 **Read.** You're going to watch a video called *Animation Creation*. Look at the storyboard on this page, and read the three sentences. Which idea do you think will be most related to the video's content? Circle the letter.

a. An animation is created more quickly than a live TV show because there's little to prepare.

b. Animations are popular because they're easy to make and cost very little money.

c. Creating animations is a process that requires careful planning and decision-making.

25 **Watch scene 7.1. While you watch, create a flowchart showing the steps for creating an animation.**

26 **After you watch, work in pairs to answer the questions.**

1. Who are the people involved in making the animation?
2. What is the purpose of a mood board?
3. What are the three stages of creating an animation?
4. What is added at the animatic stage?
5. What is the last step in creating an animation?

A storyboard

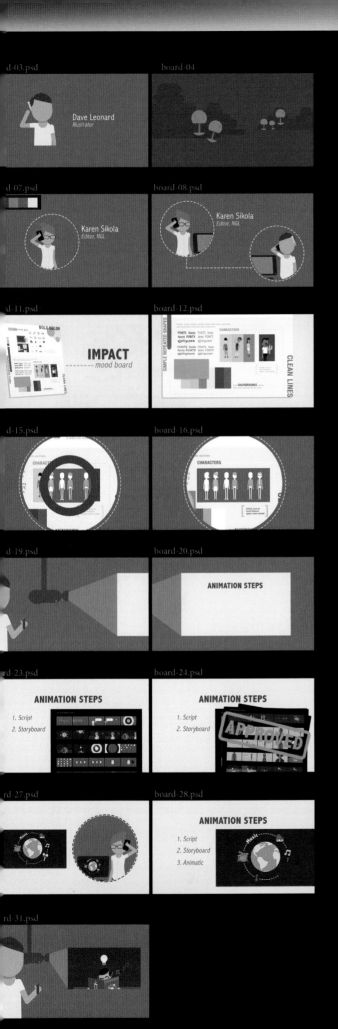

27 **Work in pairs.** In the video, the editor gives suggestions to the illustrator. What does she suggest? Check the boxes. Then discuss how each suggestion would be helpful.

- ☐ Rewrite the script.
- ☐ Use cooler colors.
- ☐ Change the style of the characters.
- ☐ Design three different storyboards.
- ☐ Change the music.

28 **Work in pairs.** Compare the steps you created in your flowchart from Activity 25. Talk about what happens at each step. Do you think this happens with all of the animations you watch? Explain.

29 **Choose an activity.**

1. **Work independently.** Imagine you're a TV producer who's looking for an illustrator to create animations for a show. Write a want ad for the job. Explain what personality traits the illustrator needs. Describe the type of work the job requires.

2. **Work in pairs.** Find an animated video online and watch it without the audio. Create a new script and choose music for the video. Then play the video for the class, using your own narration and music.

3. **Work in groups.** Research a live TV show you like and find out how it's produced. Create a Venn diagram to compare the process with the production of an animation. Present your comparison to the class.

GRAMMAR TR: 97

Reported speech: Describing what others say

"I will save my money for art supplies because I'm learning to draw manga."	She **says she will** save her money for art supplies because **she's learning** to draw manga.
	She **said she would** save her money for art supplies because **she was learning** to draw manga.
"Plan your ideas first."	The teacher **tells/is telling/told** them **to plan** their ideas first.
"Can I borrow your pencil?"	He **asked if he could** borrow my pencil.
	He asked **to borrow** my pencil.

30 **Listen.** You will hear how to draw a manga. After you listen, circle the word to correctly complete the sentences. TR: 98

1. The speaker says that you first *have / had* to plan.
2. He tells us *to choose / chose* a story.
3. He said that the next step *is / was* to create a storyboard.
4. He tells us *not to worry / don't worry* about creating a perfect storyboard.
5. He told us we *can / could* scan the drawing, but that we *will / would* need special software to edit the work.
6. Then he asked us what we *think / thought*.

31 **Work in pairs.** Listen to the audio again. Then answer the questions using reported speech. TR: 99

1. What did the speaker tell us about the process of making a manga?
   He told us it took a lot of time.

2. What did he say about creating characters?
   _____

3. What did he tell us to do after the storyboard is complete?
   _____

4. What did the speaker ask us at the end?
   _____

32 **Work in large groups.** Cut out the cards and use them to play "Telephone." Use reported speech.

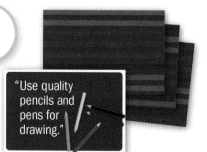

She told me to use quality pencils and pens for drawing.

"Use quality pencils and pens for drawing."

Go to p. 171.

122

WRITING

When we write stories, we often tell what others say. To do this, we can use reported speech. We can also surround the person's statement or question with quotation marks. Look at the following examples:

Annie asked if I was going to eat the apple.

"Are you going to eat the apple?" asked Annie.

Gil says it's a wonderful idea.

"It's a wonderful idea," says Gil.

33 **Read the model.** Notice how the writer quotes people in the story. Underline examples.

Whenever I look at this photo, I think of an afternoon fishing with my grandfather. My grandfather loves fishing. When we were younger, he tried to get my brother and me excited about it. "It's a wonderful way to spend the afternoon together," he told us. Every Saturday he asked us to go with him. At first we would, but fishing seemed so boring to us. Eventually, we told him that fishing wasn't our thing. After that, he would go alone.

One Saturday afternoon not long ago, I changed my mind and decided to go with him. I thought that maybe I would enjoy fishing more now that a few years have passed. So down to the water we went. We got in the water, threw the line, and waited. And waited. After three hours all we had was a single tiny fish.

"Grandpa, why do you like standing out here for hours like this?" I asked. "You've done nothing all afternoon!"

"Well," he said. "When I was a boy, fishing wasn't 'nothing.' In fact, it was everything. I didn't have TV, or video games, or smartphones. So I fished. Now, when I fish, I go back to being that boy. It was a happy time."

This photo really changed how I see my grandfather. I don't just see a quiet older man, but rather somebody who has seen many changes and has had many experiences. Looking at the photo also reminds me that my opinion of fishing changed that afternoon. Right after I took the picture, Grandpa felt a strong pull on his line. In an instant, the two of us were struggling to bring in the biggest fish I had ever seen! It was really exciting. From then on, I went fishing with him whenever I could.

34 **Work in pairs.** What story does the photo tell? How does the photo change the writer?

35 **Write.** Choose a photo of a friend or family member. Write the story your photo tells. Use reported speech and quotations to tell what people said.

Tell Stories

"It's about getting close to people, listening and looking intimately at life and the world we live in. It's about telling meaningful stories that will create awareness and hopefully inspire change for the better."

—Ami Vitale
National Geographic Photographer

1. **Watch scene 7.2.**

2. Ami Vitale uses photography to tell other people's stories. What are some ways you can find out about people's stories? How can you tell them?

3. Think of a time when someone's life changed because another person told his/her story. Summarize what happened. Then discuss why people need to tell one another's stories.

Make an Impact

A **Create a flipbook.**

· Assemble a small book. Draw on each of the pages to create animation when you flip it.

· Share your book with the class. Describe the story it tells.

· Explain the process of making your book. Answer your classmates' questions.

B **Profile a visual storyteller.**

· Go online to research visual storytellers. Select one to profile.

· Create a computer presentation about the person's life and work. Show examples of visual stories this person has told.

· Present your work to the class.

C **Tell your own visual story.**

· Think of a cause or person that is important to you. Think of the story you want to tell about this subject.

· Choose a format for your story. You might choose to draw, paint, animate, or use photographs.

· Create your visual story and share it with the class.

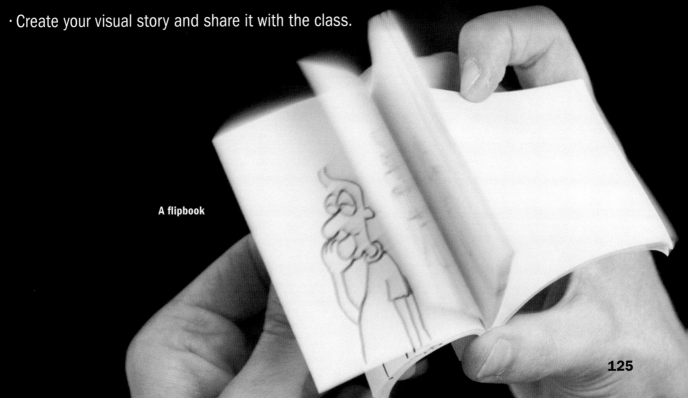

A flipbook

Unit 8

Perform and Create

"I like to think of music not just as music,
but as information."
          —Paul D. Miller, aka DJ Spooky

A performer breakdancing in a cloud of colored smoke

1. You've learned about art forms such as painting, photography, and animation. What are other ways people express themselves artistically?

2. DJ Spooky says that for him music is information. Do you agree with him? What do you learn from music?

3. What are some ways you like to express yourself?

1 **How important is music in your life? Why?**
Discuss. Then listen and read. TR: 100

Music is an essential part of many people's lives. Whether it's live or recorded, music is a **means** of **entertainment** to almost everyone. But for musicians, music is about more than just enjoyment: it's a form of **self-expression**. When we think of creating music, we think of the **composers** who write music and **lyrics** and the **performers** who play these songs. But a different kind of musical self-expression has become popular over the last few decades: being a DJ. A DJ chooses and plays pre-recorded music for an audience. He or she mixes and **manipulates** the rhythms and **beats** using different creative methods. Although the style **varies** depending on the DJ, the result is usually a high-energy sound that's perfect for dancing.

The term *DJ* comes from the words *disc* and *jockey*. The word *disc* refers to a vinyl record. Records may seem old-fashioned to people who download music from the Internet, but many DJs today still use them to spin. At a club a DJ might mix on a computer, a tablet, a turntable, or any combination of the three.

DJs don't just work at clubs. They play at events, such as weddings and birthday parties. DJs also play and discuss music on a podcast or at a radio station. In fact, DJs have been on the radio for more than a century. The very first DJ, Ray Newby, was only 16 when he played music on a small radio in 1909. Over the years, radio DJs chose what music to **expose** audiences to. Hearing their own songs on the radio brought musicians **satisfaction**. More importantly, a DJ playing your song was an indication that **fame** was on the way!

Today DJs themselves are international stars. For example, Dutch-born DJ Tiësto **gained recognition** performing at the 2004 Summer Olympics. By 2012, he was earning millions of dollars a year. Some DJs use their fame to be **influential**. For example, DJ Spooky composed the *Terra Nova/Sinfonia Antarctica* to raise awareness about environmental issues. This is not your typical symphony. This music mix is the portrait of a continent threatened by climate change. For DJ Spooky, being a DJ is more than just playing music—it's about making others think!

A DJ spinning music on a turntable

2 **Learn new words.** Listen and repeat. TR: 101

3 **Work in pairs.** Are DJs popular in your country? Have you listened to or seen a DJ perform? What's it like?

4 **Read and write the words from the list.** Make any necessary changes.

beat	composer	entertainment	influential	lyrics
manipulate	means	performer	satisfaction	vary

Paul D. Miller is a musician, writer, and _____ who performs as DJ Spooky. He's known around the world for his ability to entertain audiences by mixing hip-hop _____ . But DJ Spooky sees his complex work as much more than _____ . He sees it as a _____ of informing the public about important issues such as climate change, sustainability, and the role of technology in society. He wants his music to be _____ in changing how people think.

DJ Spooky's multimedia presentations _____ from recordings, animation, books, and videos to lectures and art installations. He even has a free, open-source app that provides other DJs with tools to mix, scratch, and add electronic effects to their own music. This way they can be _____ , too.

DJ Spooky

5 **Learn new words.** Listen to these words and match them to the definitions. Then listen and repeat. TR: 102 and 103

enjoyment	essential	indication	symphony

_____ 1. happiness or pleasure

_____ 2. necessary

_____ 3. a musical composition with many instruments

_____ 4. a sign or signal

6 **Choose an activity.**

1. **Work independently.** Think of a DJ performance you've seen, or find one online. Write a review of the performance.

2. **Work in pairs.** Discuss the following questions: Why is music important? Where and how do you listen to music? Where do you get information about new music?

3. **Work in groups.** Research a popular DJ, and find a sample of his or her recordings. Present your research to the class. Play the song clip and describe the music. Talk about the DJ's style and message.

Asking for feelings and opinions	Expressing feelings and opinions
How do you feel about <u>jazz</u>?	I'm crazy about <u>jazz</u>.
What are your thoughts on <u>hip-hop</u>?	I'm a big fan of <u>hip-hop</u>.
	It's all right, I guess.
	I'm not wild about <u>hip-hop</u>.
What do you think about <u>going to the opera</u>?	I can't stand <u>listening to opera</u>.

7 **Listen.** How do the speakers ask for and express opinions? Write the phrases you hear. TR: 105

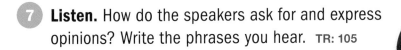

8 **Read and complete the dialogue.**

Abram: Marina, do you play an instrument?

Marina: Yes, I actually play three.

_____ music!

Abram: Me, too. _____ playing the guitar. It's how I express myself. What instruments do you play?

Marina: Well, I've been playing piano since I was four.

_____ It's not my favorite. I play the violin and the flute, too. The violin is my favorite.

Abram: Yeah, string instruments are great because you can play them anywhere. I tried to play the piano, but _____ being stuck in the house all day practicing. With my guitar I can practice wherever I go.

Marina: _____ getting together to do a song—me on the violin, you on the guitar?

Abram: Sure! We'd have to think about what musical style we'd want to work on.

Marina: _____ rock? I know some pretty cool songs with violin solos.

Abram: Sounds great!

9 **Work in groups.** Take turns. Use a coin to move. (Heads = 1 space; tails = 2 spaces) Express your feelings and opinions.

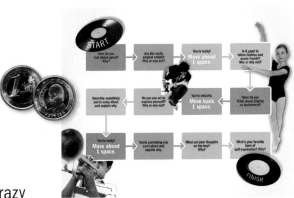

10 **Work in pairs.** Find out what you have in common. Find three things that you're both crazy about and three things you can't stand.

Go to p. 173.

131

GRAMMAR TR: 106

Gerunds and infinitives

Dancing is a popular form of self-expression.

Some people like **to perform/performing** as comedians.

Other people are interested in **acting** in videos and plays.

Building an audience of fans for a performer's work is important.

It's important **to build** an audience of fans for a performer's work.

Post information about the show on social media **to get** a big audience.

A living statue

11 **Read.** Complete the sentences with forms of the verbs in parentheses.

_____ (Express) yourself can happen in unusual ways. Some people are enthusiastic about _____ (pretend) to be statues or sculptures. They like _____ (trick) people! If the performers are outdoors, people usually walk by without _____ (realize) the statues are actually alive. Other living statues prefer _____ (work) as entertainers for companies that send them to different events and locations. And still others like _____ (enter) contests. For instance, it's the dream of many living statues _____ (win) the annual International World Championship of Living Statues. _____ (Judge) takes place in three categories: professionals, amateurs, and children.

12 **Work in pairs.** Rewrite the sentences.

1. Seeing a living statue move would surprise me.

   It _____

2. Creating an interesting look is important for a living statue.

   It _____

3. Standing still for a long time can be very difficult.

   It _____

13 **Work in groups.** Take turns creating and answering questions using the words provided with gerunds or infinitives.

> Do you ever get bored with dancing?

> No, but I get bored with watching dance shows on TV.

bored with	excited about	like	prefer

14 Learn new words. Listen to learn about dancing.
Then listen and repeat. TR: 107 and 108

A **choreographer** first plans out how a group of **ballet** dancers will dance, deciding when and how they move with the music. Then the dancers practice this dance during **rehearsal**.

Folk dancing

15 Read. Match the term to its clue.

_____ 1. folk dancing
_____ 2. choreographer
_____ 3. hip-hop dancing
_____ 4. ballet
_____ 5. rehearsal

a. a dance typically performed to classical music
b. dancing to fast, rhythmic music
c. performing a dance that's been done for generations
d. a time for working with a choreographer or director
e. a person who plans dancers' movements

16 Work in groups. Talk about different forms of artistic expression.
Use words from each box, plus a gerund or infinitive.

music composition	prefer
paint	interested in
animation	know about
dance	dislike
living statue	be essential
DJ	

I'm interested in working as a DJ. What do you think?

Well, it's essential to know a lot about music! Do you?

133

17 **Before you read, discuss in pairs.** Look at the photo. Describe what you see.

18 **Learn new words.** Find the new words below in the reading. What do you think they mean? Find antonyms for the words *freeze* and *dirty*. Then listen and repeat. TR: 109

to melt orchestra pure stage tribute

19 **While you read, draw two conclusions about the Ice Music Festival.** TR: 110

20 **After you read, work in pairs to answer the questions.**

1. Who is Terje Isungset?
2. What does Terje refer to as "art by accident"?
3. Who works together to make the instruments?
4. How are the instruments created?
5. What are three challenges facing musicians who perform at the festival?

21 **Work in pairs.** Compare the conclusions that you drew while reading with your partner's. Think of an additional conclusion you can draw about the festival.

22 **Discuss in groups.**

1. The performers at the Ice Music Festival must make music with their instruments with little rehearsal. What are the disadvantages of this process? What might the benefits be?
2. Describe a concert or music festival that you attended. What do you think organizers did to plan the event? Compare the process with that of the Ice Music Festival.
3. Would you like to attend the Ice Music Festival? Why or why not?

134

MUSIC FOR CHILLING OUT

You've never heard music *this* cool!

Winters in Norway can be long and dark, with very little sunlight. But winter can be one of the most exciting times to visit, especially for music lovers. The annual Ice Music Festival celebrates the sounds of winter. At the festival, held in the small mountain town of Geilo, world-class musicians play frozen instruments in an orchestra unlike any other.

The first Ice Music Festival took place in 2006, but its director, Terje Isungset, had been making instruments from ice since 1999. An innovative musician known for using natural elements in his instruments, Terje described discovering the capability to create sound with ice as "art by accident." Once he learned of the different sounds produced with ice, he began experimenting with a variety of instruments, including harps, horns, and xylophones. In 2005, he launched All Ice Records, a record label for ice-only music.

It's the instruments that make the Ice Music Festival unique. The process of creating them begins at a lake about 40 km (25 mi.) from Geilo. Here the ice is clean and pure, perfect for making music. The ice must be natural. Man-made ice does not produce the same sound. Workers cut 272 kg (600 lb.) blocks of ice from the lake and transport them back to town on snowmobiles. Next, ice sculptor Bill Covitz works alongside the musicians for hours to create instruments. Bill carves individual parts of each instrument, then uses water as glue to hold the parts together.

Working with ice creates new challenges for the musicians. The ice instruments are much more fragile than regular instruments. And performers can't play familiar songs because they don't know what sounds the ice instruments will make. "You cannot go on stage and expect a certain sound. You have to play with the sound that instrument actually can make. And then try to create good music out of this," says Terje. Perhaps the biggest challenge, though, is being sure that the instruments don't melt! The musicians' body heat is a threat to the instruments, especially for horn players who are blowing warm air right into the ice!

Despite the challenges, the festival brings people from around the world to hear this incredible tribute to winter, nature, and music.

A musician plays a harp made from ice.

135

VIDEO ▶

23 **Before you watch, discuss in pairs.** You're going to watch a video about *stage fright*. Based on each of the words in the phrase, what do you think stage fright is? Who do you think would have stage fright?

24 **Read and check.** The video you're going to watch is called *Stage Fright in the Spotlight*. Based on the title, predict what you'll learn. Check all that apply.

- ☐ What stage fright is
- ☐ Why it's unusual to have stage fright
- ☐ What happens when you suffer from stage fright
- ☐ How to handle stage fright
- ☐ Why you should be afraid to be onstage

25 **Watch scene 8.1. While you watch, list two ways to handle stage fright.**

26 **After you watch, work in pairs to decide if each sentence is *true* or *false*.** Check the correct answer.

1. When you suffer from stage fright, your heart might beat faster.   Ⓣ Ⓕ

2. Few people suffer from stage fright.   Ⓣ Ⓕ

3. In a survey, the only thing people fear more than talking in front of others is death.   Ⓣ Ⓕ

4. Entertainers may suffer from stage fright.   Ⓣ Ⓕ

5. Understanding why stage fright happens is important for dealing with it.   Ⓣ Ⓕ

6. Imagining the audience clapping and cheering will make you more afraid.   Ⓣ Ⓕ

27 **Work in pairs.** Think about your answer for Activity 23. Were you correct? Do you ever suffer from stage fright? If so, when? Explain what happens to you when you have to talk or perform in front of others. If not, explain how you handle speaking or performing in front of others.

28 **Discuss in groups.**

1. What do you fear most: flying, death, or speaking in front of other people? Explain your answer.

2. Tell about a time when you had to perform alone on a stage. When was it? How did you feel?

3. Think of at least two additional ways to deal with stage fright.

29 **Choose an activity.**

1. **Work independently.** Imagine you went to a performance in which the performer froze with stage fright. Write a review of the performance, including advice for the performer's next show.

2. **Work in pairs.** Role-play a dialogue between a performer and a choreographer or other trainer at a rehearsal. The performer is nervous that he will get stage fright during the performance. The trainer offers advice on what to do.

3. **Work in groups.** Find a video online of a performance where someone suffered from stage fright. Show the video to the class. Explain what happened and what the performer could have done differently.

137

GRAMMAR TR: 111

Sense verbs + infinitive: Describing what you see, hear, and feel

Did you **see the band perform** in concert?

No, but I **heard them sing** on the radio.

Come on! Let's **watch the DJ spin** records.

We'd **been hearing them practice** for days before their performance.

30 **Listen.** Write sentences in the chart about what the people did. TR: 112

	See	Hear	Feel	Watch
Jian	He saw the WagakkiBand play.			
Mei				

31 **Work independently.** Write sentences about your own experiences, using the verbs below.

1. hear / play _I've never heard the WagakkiBand play before._

2. see / dance _____

3. feel / move _____

4. watch / juggle _____

32 **Work in pairs.** Cut out the cards and take turns selecting one. Then discuss your own experiences.

> I've only ever seen an opera singer perform once. How about you?

> I saw an opera singer perform on TV.

See an opera singer perform

138

Go to p. 175.

WRITING

When we write an explanatory essay, we want to teach our reader about a topic. We must identify the topic in the first paragraph. Then we must provide additional facts, details, and examples to help the reader better understand the topic. An explanatory essay does <u>not</u> include the writer's opinion.

33 **Read the model.** The writer is teaching us about a type of puppet show. Cross out the two sentences that don't belong in the explanatory essay.

Thai puppet performances are a unique form of cultural expression. I saw a Thai puppet show and it was really awesome! In a performance, three puppeteers work together to move one beautiful, lifelike puppet to traditional music. Puppeteers must know Thai classical dance. As they dance, each puppeteer holds a wooden rod with a string attached to control different parts of the puppet.

There were different sizes and types of puppets used in Thai puppet performances throughout history, but the puppets used in modern performances are about 60 cm (2 ft.) high and made of bamboo. Their heads are very realistic, and they wear detailed, elegant costumes. In fact, the costumes are often decorated with gold and jewels. On the inside, puppets have around 16 strings that connect their body parts to one another. Moving these strings allows the puppets to move smoothly and naturally.

Puppets have been a form of entertainment in Thailand for around 300 years, but the traditional Thai puppet performances gained popularity in the early twentieth century. Master puppeteer Krae Saptawanit, who first created the small puppet in 1901, traveled around the country doing performances. However, interest in the shows decreased in the mid-twentieth century after Saptawanit's death. In 1985, a group of puppeteers formed to reintroduce the traditional art. I think this group is really good—probably better at performing the shows than the original artists. Today these puppet shows are popular with local people and tourists alike!

34 **Work in pairs.** What did you learn about the art of Thai puppetry? Would you like to see a performance? Why or why not?

35 **Write.** Write an essay to explain a type of artistic expression. Remember to provide facts, details, and examples to teach your reader about the topic.

139

Do Your Own Thing

"There are so many people who just let the world define them. What happens when you begin to realize another world is possible—that's art."

—Paul D. Miller, aka DJ Spooky

National Geographic Explorer, Artist/Writer/Musician

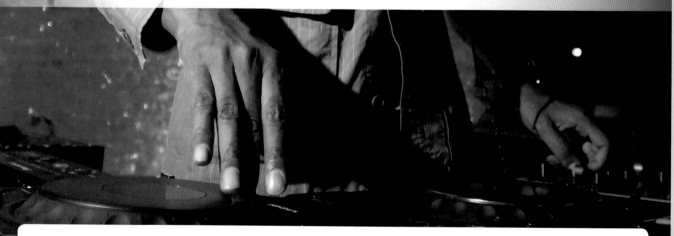

1. **Watch scene 8.2.**

2. What would you say your "own thing" is? How does it bring you closer to other people? How does it help you stand out?

3. Do you let the world define you? Or do you define who you are? Or both? Explain with examples.

Make an Impact

A Perform for your class.

· Choose a type of performing art to perform for the class.

· Before you perform, explain what you're going to do. Give background on the history and popularity of your performing art form. Talk about what you need to know and have to perform.

· Hold a question-and-answer session with the class after your performance.

B Interview a performer.

· Think of a performing artist in your community. Prepare ten questions to ask the artist about the type of work he or she does.

· Conduct your interview. Audio record or film it.

· Play your interview for the class.

C Make a timeline.

· Choose a type of performing art. Research its history.

· Make a timeline to illustrate the history of this performing art. Use photos to show how it's changed.

· Present your timeline to the class.

Express Yourself

1 **Look at and listen to the presentation.** TR: 113

NOT
Your Typical
Performance

Makeup

Costumes

A visual story

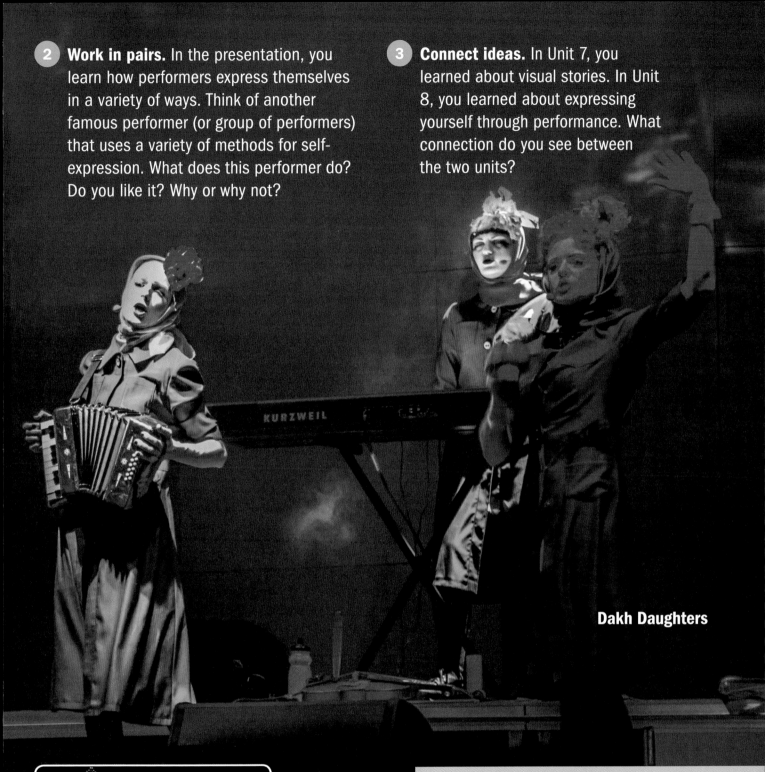

2 **Work in pairs.** In the presentation, you learn how performers express themselves in a variety of ways. Think of another famous performer (or group of performers) that uses a variety of methods for self-expression. What does this performer do? Do you like it? Why or why not?

3 **Connect ideas.** In Unit 7, you learned about visual stories. In Unit 8, you learned about expressing yourself through performance. What connection do you see between the two units?

Dakh Daughters

A variety of instruments

4 **Choose an activity.**

1. Choose a topic:
   - visual stories
   - performances

2. Choose a way to express yourself:
   - a storyboard or animation
   - a computer presentation
   - a performance

3. Present your work.

143

Unit 1

Intonation in tag questions

1 **Listen.** Notice how the voice goes up or down in the tag question. TR: 114

He seems shy, doesn't he?

The voice goes down in the tag. In this case, the speaker is sure or almost sure.

You're not jealous, are you?

The voice goes up in the tag. In this case, the speaker is less sure.

2 **Listen and repeat.** Does the voice go up or down? Mark it with an arrow. Then circle the tags where the speaker is sure. TR: 115

1. Your friends aren't very open-minded, are they?
2. Your sisters are very competitive, aren't they?
3. You didn't go to the party on Saturday, did you?
4. Your sister was at the party, wasn't she?
5. You were very self-conscious when you were younger, weren't you?
6. You've become more self-confident, haven't you?

3 **Work in pairs.** Listen and repeat each sentence. Then take turns repeating the tag questions and answering them. TR: 116

You love school, don't you?   Yes, I do!

1. You love school, don't you? (sure)
2. English is easy, isn't it? (sure)
3. Your town has a soccer team, doesn't it? (not sure)
4. Your family is big, isn't it? (not sure)
5. You don't have a pet, do you? (sure)

Unit 2

Modals + *have* + past participle

1 **Listen.** Notice how *have* is pronounced after modals. TR: 117

They could have read about it.
He might have seen a jellyfish.
She must have been scared.

Have is often reduced. It sounds like the word *of.*

2 **Listen and repeat.** Be sure to reduce *have*. TR: 118

1. She might have seen a spider.
2. They must have been afraid.
3. He could have read about the bear.
4. They could have been fire ants.
5. It might have been a rat.

3 **Work in pairs.** Take turns responding to the statements. Use *could / might / must* + *have* and the phrase in parentheses. Reduce *have*.

Gina just screamed.   She must have seen a cockroach.

1. A: Gina just screamed. (B: seen a cockroach)
2. A: Lee and Sue are afraid. (B: heard about the snakes)
3. A: Ray doesn't want to swim. (B: known about the sharks)
4. A: I was stung by a wasp! (B: been near its nest)
5. A: Julian went home. (B: felt sick)
6. A: Ann likes pit bulls. (B: read about them)

Unit 3
Pausing

1 **Listen.** Notice the short pauses between the groups of words that go together. TR: 119

She's scared of wasps, / so we stayed in.
As a result, / we didn't go hiking.

In writing, pauses are often signaled by punctuation such as commas or periods. But this is not always the case. Listen to this example. Notice the pause.

We stayed in / because he was scared.

Pausing will help your speech to be clear and easy to understand.

2 **Listen and repeat.** Draw a line where you hear a pause. TR: 120

1. In my class, we often work in groups.
2. Students work hard, so they should get a break.
3. When I see a spider, I scream.
4. I don't like ants because they seem dirty.
5. I like elephants because they have complex emotions.

3 **Work in pairs.** Take turns completing the sentences using your own ideas. Add pauses when you speak. Your partner will respond. When you finish, switch roles.

> In my class, I ask a lot of questions. Me, too!

1. In my class, _____ .
2. Students work hard, so they _____ .
3. When I see a spider, _____ .

Unit 4
Shouldn't have + past participle

1 **Listen.** Notice how *not have* is pronounced after *should*. TR: 121

You shouldn't have thrown it away.
I shouldn't have washed it.

Not have or the contracted *n't* is often reduced to sound like *en*. The *t* sound is often silent. *Have* sounds like the word *of*. There is just a small difference between the negative and positive forms. Listen closely.

He should have bought it.
He shouldn't have bought it.

2 **Listen.** Circle the form you hear. Then listen again and repeat. TR: 122

1. A: Oh, I (should / shouldn't) have bought this shirt.
   B: You (should / shouldn't) have cut the tags off. Now you can't return it!

2. A: You (should / shouldn't) have gone to the mall. You (should / shouldn't) have tried that new thrift store I told you about.
   B: Oh, I forgot! You (should / shouldn't) have reminded me.

3 **Work in pairs.** Take turns practicing the conversations with your partner. Use *shouldn't have* and the words in parentheses.

1. A: I'm so tired today! (B: gone to bed so late)
2. A: I ruined my jeans! (B: washed them in hot water)
3. A: I failed the test! (B: missed class so much)
4. A: He made me late! (B: waited for him)

> I'm so tired today! You shouldn't have gone to bed so late.

Unit 5
Past perfect

1 **Listen.** Notice how *had* sounds in the past perfect. TR: 123

A: Had anyone tried to fly before the Wright brothers?

B: Yes, I think flying had been attempted by many people.

A: Until the class, Tim had never realized that bats are mammals.

B: I hadn't either!

When *had* comes after the subject or a question word, the pronunciation is often contracted *'d* or reduced.

The word *had* is not reduced when it comes at the beginning of a question, in a negative statement, or in a short answer. The vowel sound is clearly pronounced.

2 **Listen and repeat.** Circle the two reduced examples of *had*. TR: 124

1. A: Who had never seen a bat up close?
   B: I hadn't. They're so cute!

2. Cindy had always wanted to learn about birds.

3. A: Had you seen a bat before, Matt?
   B: Yes, I had. But I hadn't realized they were mammals.

3 **Work in pairs.** Listen and complete the conversation with *had* or *hadn't*. Circle each reduced *had*. Then practice the conversation. TR: 125

A. Some ancient bird fossils are missing. The guard ⟨had⟩ just finished his breakfast when he heard something downstairs. But all he found was the case open and the fossils missing.

B: _____ anyone signed in?

A: No, no one _____ signed in, but someone _____ been in there.

B: OK, talk to anyone who might've seen something.

A: Yes. We will. One student _____ been studying near the door at the time, but says he _____ been paying attention.

Unit 6
Final *d* + *you*

1 **Listen.** Notice how the final *d* links with the *y* in *you*. TR: 126

Would‿you go to Mars?
       j

Could‿you help me with my essay?
      j

Did‿you know that Mars had water?
    j

Who told‿you about Space Camp?
         j

When the final *d* links with the *y*, it forms a *j* sound (as in **j**uice).

2 **Listen and repeat.** Draw an arrow to link the final *d* words to *you*. TR: 127

1. Where did you go on your last vacation?
2. If you could, would you go to the moon?
3. Who called you or texted you last week?
4. Did you get a good grade on your last test?
5. What did you do last weekend?

3 **Work in pairs.** Take turns asking and answering the questions in Activity 2. Be sure to link the *d* and *y* sounds.

> Where did you go on your last vacation?

> I went to the mountains with my family.

> What did you do there?

> We went skiing.

Unit 7

Dropped *h*

1 **Listen.** Listen for the *h* sound. Can you hear it? TR: 128

Ami Vitale tells stories with ~~h~~er photos.

He asked if ~~h~~e could take ~~h~~er portrait.

She told ~~h~~im she wanted to be a poet.

When the words *he, him, his,* and *her* come after another word in the same phrase, the *h* sound is often dropped.

2 **Read.** Cross out possible dropped *h* sounds. Then listen and repeat. TR: 129

1. His teacher told him to take the photo again.
2. Did you tell her that her photo won the contest?
3. I'm not sure if he finished his painting.
4. Her photos of her hometown were beautiful.
5. Tell him that he has to finish her portrait today.

3 **Work in pairs.** Cross out possible dropped *h* sounds. Listen and repeat. Then practice the conversation. TR: 130

A: Did Pete ask Jim about his plans this weekend?

B: He asked him if he wanted to work on the animation project.

A: What did he say?

B: He said yes, but first he had to help his mother fix her car.

Unit 8

Rhythm and stress

1 **Listen.** Notice the rhythm. TR: 131

● ● ●
mu **si** cian

You **miss** him.

Stressed words or syllables create a strong beat. The rhythm of English depends on the number of strong beats, not the number of words. Listen to these sentences. The rhythm is the same for each.

●   ●   ●
Joe   **plays**   **drums**.

Joe can   **play** the **drums**.

Joe is   **play**ing the **drums**.

Joe has   been **play**ing the **drums**.

Joe should've been **play**ing the **drums**.

The unstressed words are often shortened to keep the rhythm.

2 **Listen.** Listen and repeat sentences *a* and *b*. Clap to the rhythm. Then listen to sentences 1–5 and match the rhythm pattern. Write *a* or *b*. TR: 132

●   ●   ● ● ●
a. I'm **cra**zy about **jazz**.   b. I **can't stand op**era.

1. __*a*__ Her **mu**sic is **great**.
2. _____ I **felt** the **ground shake**.
3. _____ Is he **go**ing to the **show**?
4. _____ I **saw** the **band play**.
5. _____ Her **voice** is **beau**tiful.

3 **Work in pairs.** Listen and repeat the dialogues. Then practice them, adding your ideas. Use correct rhythm. TR: 133

I can **play** a **mu**sical **in**strument.   **What in**strument?   The **gui**tar.

1. A: I can **play** a **mu**sical **in**strument.   B: **What in**strument?

2. A: I **can't play** _____ .   B: **That's too bad.**

3. A: I'm **cra**zy about this **band**.   B: **What band** is it?

Irregular Verbs

Infinitive	Simple past	Past participle	Infinitive	Simple past	Past participle
be	were	been	leave	left	left
beat	beat	beaten	lend	lent	lent
become	became	become	let	let	let
begin	began	begun	lie (down)	lay	lain
bend	bent	bent	light	lit	lit
bet	bet	bet	lose	lost	lost
bite	bit	bitten	make	made	made
bleed	bled	bled	mean	meant	meant
blow	blew	blown	meet	met	met
break	broke	broken	overcome	overcame	overcome
bring	brought	brought	pay	paid	paid
build	built	built	put	put	put
burn	burned/burnt	burned/burnt	quit	quit	quit
buy	bought	bought	read	read	read
carry	carried	carried	ride	rode	ridden
catch	caught	caught	ring	rang	rung
choose	chose	chosen	rise	rose	risen
come	came	come	run	ran	run
cost	cost	cost	say	said	said
cut	cut	cut	see	saw	seen
deal	dealt	dealt	sell	sold	sold
dig	dug	dug	send	sent	sent
dive	dove/dived	dived	set	set	set
do	did	done	sew	sewed	sewn
draw	drew	drawn	shake	shook	shaken
drink	drank	drunk	shine	shone	shone
drive	drove	driven	show	showed	shown
dry	dried	dried	shrink	shrank	shrunk
eat	ate	eaten	shut	shut	shut
fall	fell	fallen	sing	sang	sung
feed	fed	fed	sink	sank	sunk
feel	felt	felt	sit	sat	sat
fight	fought	fought	sleep	slept	slept
find	found	found	slide	slid	slid
flee	fled	fled	speak	spoke	spoken
fly	flew	flown	spend	spent	spent
forbid	forbade	forbidden	spin	spun	spun
forget	forgot	forgotten	stand	stood	stood
forgive	forgave	forgiven	steal	stole	stolen
freeze	froze	frozen	stick	stuck	stuck
fry	fried	fried	sting	stung	stung
get	got	gotten	stink	stank	stunk
give	gave	given	strike	struck	struck/stricken
go	went	gone	swear	swore	sworn
grind	ground	ground	sweep	swept	swept
grow	grew	grown	swim	swam	swum
hang	hung	hung	swing	swung	swung
have	had	had	take	took	taken
hear	heard	heard	teach	taught	taught
hide	hid	hidden	tear	tore	torn
hit	hit	hit	tell	told	told
hold	held	held	think	thought	thought
hurt	hurt	hurt	throw	threw	thrown
keep	kept	kept	understand	understood	understood
kneel	knelt/kneeled	knelt/kneeled	wake	woke	woken
knit	knitted/knit	knitted/knit	wear	wore	worn
know	knew	known	weave	wove/weaved	woven/weaved
lay	laid	laid	win	won	won
lead	led	led	write	wrote	written

Two-word Verbs – Inseparable

Verb	Meaning	Sample sentence
amount to	be the same as; turn out to be	The total **amounts to** five hundred. Some people thought he would not **amount to** anything, but he became famous.
apply for	to make a request	Do you plan to **apply for** a summer job?
apply to	be relevant	The rules **apply to** everyone!
ask around	ask several people	I'll **ask around** in case anyone found a lost phone.
break down	stop functioning	The car **broke down** yesterday.
break up	end a relationship	Did you hear that Lara and Renato **broke up**?
calm down	relax after being angry	**Calm down**! Everything will be OK.
check in	register at a hotel or airport	We can't **check in** until one o'clock.
check out	leave a hotel	He **checked out** at 10:20 and went straight to the airport.
cheer up	become happier	**Cheer up**! I'm sure your team will do better next time.
come across	find unexpectedly	I **came across** a very interesting article about crocodiles.
come from	originate in	Mangoes originally **come from** Asia.
count on	rely on	Please be there on time. I'm **counting on** you!
dress up	wear nice clothes	Mom, do I really need to **dress up** for the party?
eat out	eat at a restaurant	Why don't we **eat out** on Friday?
end up	eventually do/decide	We **ended up** going to the movies last night.
engage in	take part in	The principal **engaged in** talks with the student council.
fall apart	break into pieces	Mom, I need a new desk. This one's **falling apart**.
fall down	fall to the ground	I **fell down** and broke my ankle!
find out	learn	I was so excited when I **found out** we were going to Spain!
fit in	blend in; belong because you're similar	Teenagers wear certain clothes to **fit in**.
get along	be friendly with someone	I really like Tom. We **get along** well.
get over	recover from a problem	I know she's upset you didn't call her, but she'll **get over** it.
get together	meet; gather	Let's **get together** on Wednesday after school!
get up	get out of bed; rise	I **get up** at seven o'clock every day.
give in	surrender; quit	I won't **give in** to pressure from my friends.
give up	stop trying	Don't **give up**. This puzzle is too hard.
go ahead	do; begin to do	Why don't you **go ahead** and invite her to the party?
go back	return	He **went back** to the site and discovered a second dinosaur.
go over	review	Let's **go over** the presentation before class.
grow up	become an adult	I **grew up** in China.
hang in	stay positive	**Hang in** there. I'm sure you'll find the phone.
hang on	wait	**Hang on** a minute. I'm on the phone.
hang out	spend time	Do you want to **hang out** on Saturday?
hold on	wait	**Hold on** a second! I think I found the answer.
lead to	cause to happen	His research **led to** the discovery of a new species.

Verb	Meaning	Sample sentence
light up	become bright	The sky **lit up** with fireworks.
log in/on	sign in to a website or app	I can't **log in** because I don't remember my password.
look after	take care of	I have to **look after** my little sister this Sunday.
look back	think about things that happened in the past	**Looking back,** I think the other project topic was more interesting.
look for	try to find	What are you **looking for**? Did you lose anything?
look into	try to find out about	I need to **look into** it. I'll let you know tomorrow.
not care for	not like	I do**n't** really **care for** opera.
pass away	die	I heard Kim's grandma **passed away**.
prey on	hunt and kill for food	Do lions **prey on** zebras?
rave about	talk or write very enthusiastically	Critics are **raving about** the new film.
rely on	trust; depend on	Do you think we **rely on** technology too much?
run away	escape; leave	Our dog **ran away**!
run into	meet unexpectedly; collide	Yesterday I **ran into** my first grade teacher. I **ran into** a tree.
stand out	be noticeable	I was the only one wearing purple. I really **stood out**.
take off	start to fly	The flight **took off** on time.
turn out	result; happen	I thought everyone in my family had a cell phone. It **turns out** my uncle refuses to get one!
wake up	stop sleeping	I usually **wake up** at six o'clock.
warm up	prepare for exercise	Do you **warm up** before soccer games?
work out	be successful; exercise	Everyone liked our presentation. It **worked out** well! I prefer to **work out** in the gym when it's cold.

Two-word Verbs – Separable

Verb	Meaning	Sample sentence
back up	support	His friends **backed** him **up**.
call off	cancel	They had planned a party, but they had to **call** it **off**.
calm down	help relax	Let's play soft music to **calm** the baby **down**.
carry out	do or complete something	They are **carrying out** research on ancient birds.
check out	observe; notice	**Check out** my new phone!
cheer up	try to make someone happy	Why don't we get some flowers to **cheer** her **up**?
clean up	organize; clean	Can you **clean** that **up**? Guests are arriving soon.
cut down	make something fall to the ground	They're **cutting down** too many trees.
cut off	remove by cutting	Did you read about that hiker that had to **cut off** his own arm?
do over	do again	My brother spilled soda on my poster, so I had to **do** it **over**!
draw in	capture the interest	This book really **drew** me **in**.
equip with	supply with	They **equipped** the astronauts **with** extra oxygen tanks.
figure out	find the answer; solve	He finally **figured** it **out**.
fill out	write information in a form	Remember to **fill out** the form before the end of the week.

Verb	Meaning	Sample sentence
fill up	fill to the top	Don't **fill up** the cup. I need room for milk.
find out	discover information	How did you **find** that **out**?
get across	make understandable	We need to add more examples to **get** the idea **across**!
give back	return something	Do you still have my book? Can you **give** it **back** to me?
give up	quit (a habit)	I'm **giving up** coffee!
hand in	submit	Did you **hand in** the homework in time?
hand out	distribute	I'll make copies and **hand** them **out**.
let down	disappoint	I really want you to come to the party. Don't **let** me **down**.
let in	allow to come in	They didn't **let** him **in** with his backpack.
light up	make bright	At night the stars **light** the sky **up**.
look up	find information	Can you **look** it **up** in a dictionary?
make up	lie about; invent	That can't be true. I think he **made** it **up**.
mix up	confuse things or people	They always **mix** me **up** with my sister.
put off	postpone	Can we **put off** the meeting until next week?
put together	assemble	Can you help me **put** this **together**?
take down	remove	They **took down** the painting because it was controversial.
take off	remove	**Take off** that coat. You'll be too hot.
take over	gain control of	He **took over** the company when his father died.
throw away	put in the garbage; get rid of	Don't **throw away** plastic bottles. Recycle them.
track down	find after a long search	I'm trying to **track down** a friend from first grade.
try on	put on to see if it fits	I **tried on** my sister's shoes, but they didn't fit.
turn away	reject; refuse to admit	He applied to ten schools, but eight **turned** him **away**.
turn down	decrease the strength	**Turn** the TV **down** a bit. It's too loud.
turn off	power off	Don't forget to **turn off** the lights when you leave.
turn on	power on	**Turn on** the TV. The game has started!
turn up	increase the strength	I can't hear. Can you **turn up** the volume?
warm up	make warmer	Can you **warm up** the milk?
work out	find a solution	I'm sure you'll **work** it **out**.

Three-word Verbs – Inseparable

Verb	Meaning	Sample sentence
add up to	become a certain amount; result in something	The total **adds up to** two hundred.
break up with	end a relationship	She **broke up with** her boyfriend last week.
come down with	get sick	He **came down with** a cold.
come up against	face; confront	He **came up against** many obstacles during his research.
come up with	think of; find a solution	She **came up with** an excellent plan.
cut down on	use less of; do less	You should **cut down on** so much screen time!
get along with	be friendly with	My sister **gets along with** everyone!
get around to	find time to finally do	I finally **got around to** writing holiday cards.
get away with	not get caught	How did you **get away with** not doing the homework?
get back into	become interested again	I stopped playing soccer two years ago, but then I **got back into** it.

Verb	Meaning	Sample sentence
get out of	avoid doing something you don't want to do	I think that's just an excuse to **get out of** doing the project!
give up on	lose hope that somebody or something will succeed	I **gave up on** trying to become an athlete.
grow out of	change your mind over time; become too big for	He wants to be a rock star, but I'm sure he'll **grow out of** it. You'll **grow out of** that jacket before winter is over!
look down on	feel that somebody is less important	Many people **looked down on** him and his art, but he went on to become a famous artist.
look forward to	be excited about (something in the future)	I **look forward to** going on vacation.
look out for	protect; take care of	He's very selfish! He only **looks out for** himself.
look up to	have a lot of respect for	Many kids **look up to** athletes or pop stars.
play around with	try several options	I **played around with** it until I found the problem!
put up with	tolerate	Our teacher doesn't **put up with** bad behavior.
run out of	use everything	I think we've **run out of** milk. Can you get some?
stand up for	defend	Don't let him make fun of you. **Stand up for** yourself!
watch out for	be alert; anticipate	**Watch out for** deer crossing the road!

Verbs followed by infinitives and gerunds

Verbs followed by infinitive

He **agreed to go**.

afford	deserve	offer
agree	fail	plan
appear	happen	pretend
arrange	hesitate	refuse
attempt	hope	seem
care	intend	tend
claim	learn	vow
decide	manage	wait
demand		

Verbs followed by infinitive or noun/pronoun + infinitive

He **wants to learn** French.
I **want him to learn** French.

ask	prepare
choose	promise
dare	want
expect	wish
need	would like

Verbs followed by noun/pronoun + infinitive

I **convinced her to try** sushi.

cause	motivate
challenge	order
convince	persuade
empower	remind
forbid	tell
force	urge
hire	warn
invite	

Verbs followed by gerund or noun/pronoun + infinitive

They don't **allow surfing** here.
They didn't **allow him to surf** here.

advise
allow
encourage
permit
require

Verbs followed by a gerund

You should **avoid swimming** there.

admit	delay	imagine	mind	report
anticipate	deny	involve	miss	resist
appreciate	discuss	justify	postpone	risk
avoid	dislike	keep	practice	suggest
can't help	enjoy	look forward to	put off	understand
carry on	feel like	mention	recommend	
consider	finish			

Verbs followed by infinitive or gerund (similar meaning)

I **hate waking** up early.
I **hate to wake** up early.

begin	hate	prefer
can't bear	like	propose
can't stand	love	start
continue		

Verbs followed by infinitive or gerund (different meaning)

I **remember going** there last year.
I **remembered to go** to the store.

forget	remember
go on	stop
quit	try
regret	

Start

Compare

Contrast two of your teachers.

You're lucky! Move ahead 2 spaces.

You're stubborn! Move back 1 space.

Contrast two favorite TV characters.

Compare

Compare yourself and your best friend.

Contrast

You're energetic! Move ahead 2 spaces.

Congratulations! You're finished!

Compare yourself and a brother, sister, or cousin.

Contrast

End

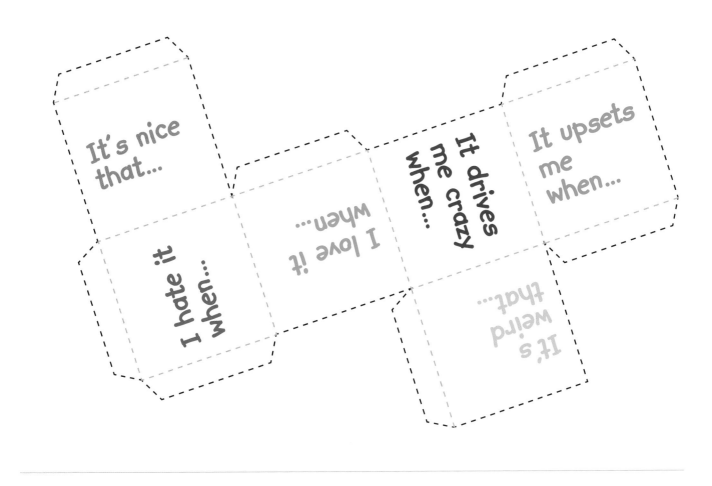

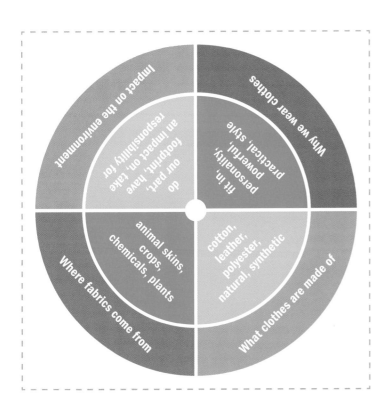

true — Giraffes clean their ears with their tongues.	**true** — Sharks grow around 30,000 teeth in their lifetime.	**false** — Camels don't sweat, so their humps are full of water.	**true** — Rats clean themselves frequently. They even wash their faces with water.
true — Kangaroos can't walk backward.	**true** — A bird called the Egyptian plover goes inside a crocodile's mouth to clean its teeth—and then flies out safely.	**true** — Crocodiles can't stick out their tongues.	**false** — Hippos sweat a red-pink version of blood.
false — Polar bears cover their black noses with a paw when they want to hide in the snow.	**true** — Some octopuses can be poisonous.	**true** — The mantis shrimp has a special front arm that can heat surrounding water up to 4,700°C (8,500°F).	**true** — The giant Goliath bird-eater spider can cover the head of a man.

Start

Make a sentence about army ants.

Use: **Because of**

You're lucky!

Move forward 3 spaces.

Make a sentence about schools of fish and predators.

Use: **As a result**

End

Make a sentence about cockroaches.

Use: **So**

Make a sentence about elephant group behavior.

Use: **Since**

Make a sentence about yourself and a friend.

Use: **So**

You're unlucky!

Move back 1 space.

Make a sentence about yourself and a family member.

Use: **Since**

You're unlucky!

Move back 1 space.

Make a sentence about bees and wasps.

Use: **Consequently**

Make a sentence about yourself.

Use: **Because**

Make a sentence about monkeys.

Use: **Because of**

Make a sentence about yourself.

Use: **As a result**

Make a sentence about groups of birds flying together.

Use: **Due to**

Make a sentence about mosquitoes.

Use: **Due to**

You're unlucky!

Move back 1 space.

START

Your friend bought another pair of sneakers—for a total of 14.

Your little brother always takes your favorite hat without asking.

You have a small fashion footprint! **Advance 2 spaces.**

Your sister washed your favorite white dress with a load of black clothes.

Your friend borrowed your new jeans without asking.

Your brother got chocolate ice cream all over your favorite shirt.

You don't think before you buy! **Go back 2 spaces.**

Your dad always throws out old ties he never wears anymore.

You do your part to protect the planet. **Advance 2 spaces.**

Your aunt isn't interested in reducing her fashion footprint.

You don't recycle old clothing! **Go back 2 spaces.**

A classmate forgot to collect clothes for the recycling party.

FINISH

Insects evolved from ancient animals that lived in water.

Argue YES or NO.

Pterosaurs were too big to generate powered flight, so they just glided.

Argue YES or NO.

Contagious behavior such as yawning can sometimes cross species.

Argue YES or NO.

Hollow bones in pterosaurs and birds reduced weight and supported wings in flight.

Argue YES or NO.

Bats evolved from large dinosaurs that lived on the ground.

Argue YES or NO.

Over millions of years in the future, flight may eventually evolve in humans.

Argue YES or NO.

Flight evolved because it helped creatures find new sources of food and escape predators.

Argue YES or NO.

All birds that fly have wings, but not all birds that have wings fly.

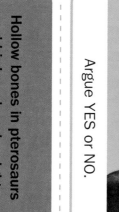

Argue YES or NO.

Birth order is the best way to understand your personality.

Argue YES or NO.

Feathers appeared before flight and helped control body temperature.

Argue YES or NO.

Cockroaches are as careful about being clean as cats are.

Argue YES or NO.

Cotton plants need only small amounts of pesticides, water, and energy to produce crops used in clothing.

Argue YES or NO.

163

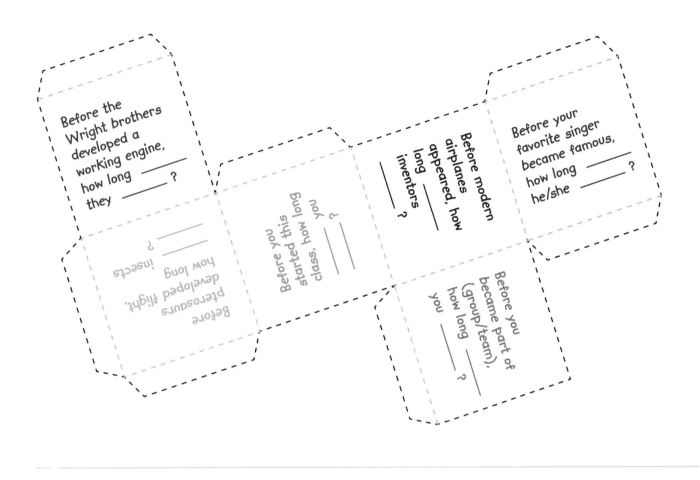

Before the Wright brothers developed a working engine, how long _____ they _____ ?

Before pterosaurs developed flight, how long _____ insects _____ ?

Before you started this class, how long _____ you _____ ?

Before modern airplanes appeared, how long _____ inventors _____ ?

Before your favorite singer became famous, how long _____ he/she _____ ?

Before you became part of (group/team), how long _____ you _____ ?

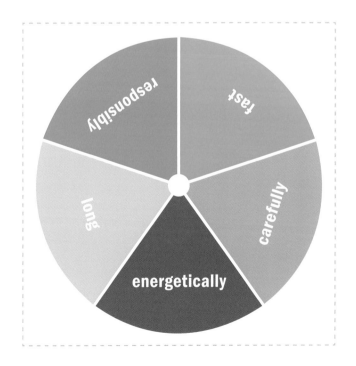

responsibly
fast
carefully
long
energetically

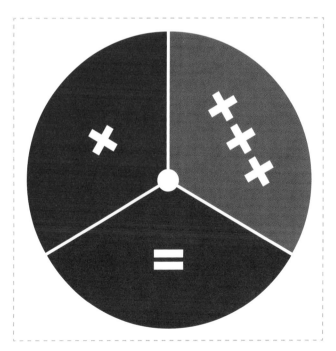

✕
✕✕✕
＝

Water flowing
on Mars

The surface
of Mars, in the Valles
Marineris area

A sand dune
on Mars

An illustration
of a dust storm
on Mars

Round balls
of minerals found
on Mars

Curiosity Rover
exploring Mars

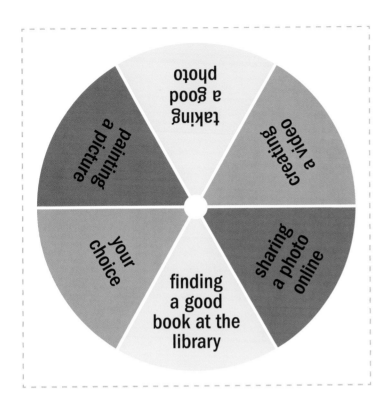

"Can you tell a visual story?"

"Ami Vitale tells stories with her photos."

"Use quality pencils and pens for drawing."

"Stop reading so many comic books."

"I prefer realistic art to abstract art."

"Videos are one way to tell a story."

"I will learn to create animations."

"Do you like manga?"

"Illustrators change their work many times before publishing it."

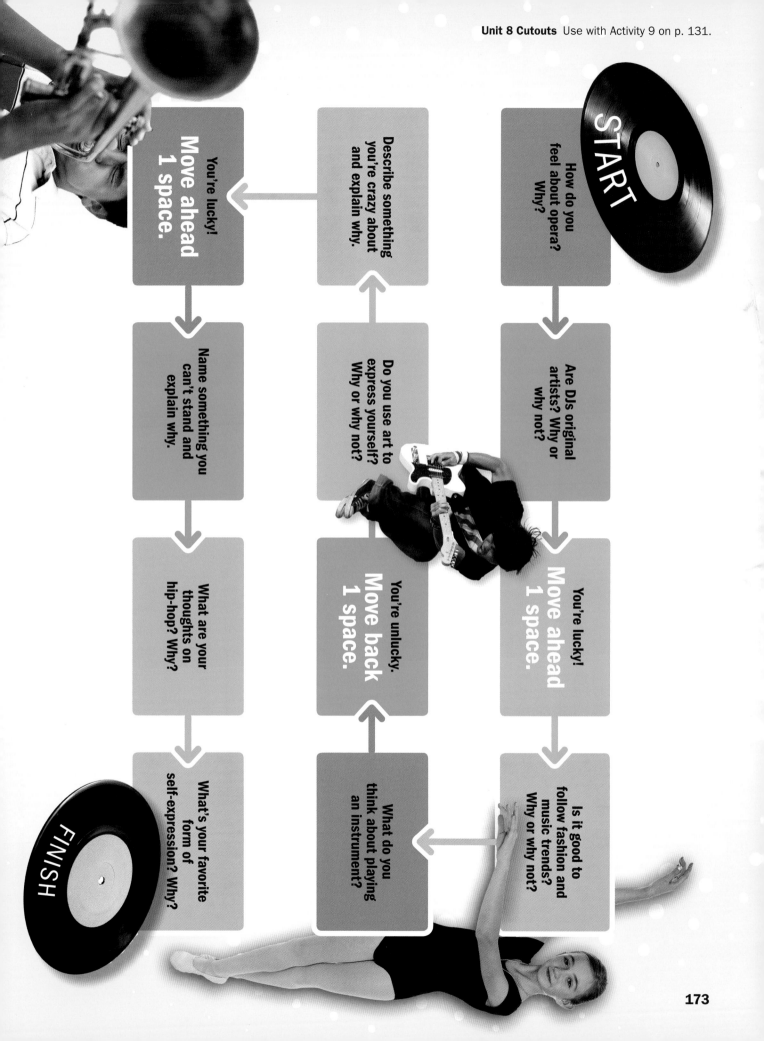

START

How do you feel about opera? Why?

Are DJs original artists? Why or why not?

You're lucky! Move ahead 1 space.

Is it good to follow fashion and music trends? Why or why not?

What do you think about playing an instrument?

You're unlucky. Move back 1 space.

Do you use art to express yourself? Why or why not?

Describe something you're crazy about and explain why.

You're lucky! Move ahead 1 space.

Name something you can't stand and explain why.

What are your thoughts on hip-hop? Why?

What's your favorite form of self-expression? Why?

FINISH